*Saudi-Iranian Relations
1932-1982*

Saudi–Iranian Relations
1932–1982

Saeed M. Badeeb

Centre for Arab
and Iranian Studies
and
Echoes

British Library Cataloguing-in-Publication Data
A Catalogue record for this book is available from the
British Library

ISBN 1 873395 04 3

First published 1993 by
Centre for Arab and Iranian Studies
5 Streatham Street
London WC1A 1JB
and
Echoes
26 Westbourne Grove
London W2 5RH

© Saeed M. Badeeb 1993

Typeset by Group E, London

Contents

List of Tables and Figures	7
Acknowledgements	9
List of Abbreviations and Acronyms	11
Glossary	12
Foreword *by David E. Long*	13
Introduction	15
1. Historical Background, 1925–32	19
The Security Dimension	22
Internal Security	23
External Security	25
The Religious Dimension	31
The Political Dimension	35
2. A Comparison of the Political Systems	37
The Saudi Political System	37
The Iranian Political System	39
Monarchical Systems	41
Cabinets and Councils of Ministers	42
Parliament	42
Religious Institutions	43
The Judiciary Systems	43
Regional Government and Political Parties	44
3. Foreign Policy and Bilateral Foreign Relations, 1932–82	47
A Period of Ups and Downs (1932–41)	47
New Directions, New Problems (1941–53)	50
The Era of Give and Take (1953–64)	52
The Era of Competition and Friendship (1964–75)	57
The Decade of Mutual Understanding (the 1970s)	62
The Gulf Islands	62
Oil	63
The Communist Threat	65
4. The Religious Relationship, 1924–82	69
Understanding Islam	70
Saudi Arabia and Islam	74
Iran and Islam	76
Saudi Arabia, Iran and Islam	79
Differences in the Practice of Islam	82
The Grand Pilgrimage (*Hajj*)	82

Contents

Prayer (*Salat*) and Other Religious Issues	86
Islamic Solidarity	87
The Issue of Islamic Solidarity	87
The Creation of Islamic Institutions	88
Religious Relations (1979–82)	90
Conclusion	92
5. Economic Relations, 1932–82	**93**
Historical Overview	93
Saudi Arabia: A Brief Economic Overview	94
Iran: A Brief Economic Overview	98
Economic Relations	101
The Early Years (1924–41)	101
The Developmental Years (1941–60)	104
The Contemporary Period (1960–82)	107
6. Military Relations, 1932–82	**115**
Confrontational Issues	118
Arabistan	118
Bahrain and the Gulf Islands Dispute	119
The Median Line Dispute	121
The Arab–Israeli Problem	122
Gulf Regional Security	123
Co-operation Issues	126
The 1957 Proposed Military Pact	128
The 1962 Yemen Civil War	129
The Dhufar Rebellion in Oman	129
Intelligence Co-operation	130
Appendix I. Friendship Treaty between the Kingdom of the Hijaz, Najd and its Dependencies and the Kingdom of Persia, 1929	133
Appendix II. Text of Joint Communiqué at the Conclusion of the Visit of His Imperial Majesty the Shahinshah of Iran to Saudi Arabia, 1957	136
Appendix III. Commercial Agreement between the Kingdom of Saudi Arabia and the Kingdom of Iran, 1971	137
Notes	139
Index of Names	157

Tables and Figures

Tables
1. Saudi Arabia and Iran: a Comparative Chart of Means and Methods during the Early Stages of Nation-building — 32
2. The Six Major Institutions of the Saudi Political Structure — 40
3. No. of Iranian Pilgrims who Made the *Hajj*, 1961–87 — 84
4. Iran's Imports from Saudi Arabia, 1969–74 — 93
5. Iran's Non-oil Exports to Saudi Arabia, 1969–74 — 93

Figures
1. State of Saudi–Iranian Relations, 1930–80 — 68
2. Iran–Israel Economic Exchange, 1958 — 106
3. Iran–Israel Economic Exchange, 1966 — 106

Acknowledgements

As the Arabs say, 'He who does not thank people does not thank Allah.' I have quoted this famous saying to express my thanks and gratitude to all those who extended to me their hands and helped me bring this piece of work to its conclusion. Once the idea of writing the book came to my mind, I received many encouraging words from a wide range of friends who supported me with their thoughts and ideas and provided me with some extremely valuable documents.

Among the very special supporters is Dr David E. Long, my chief editor and the writer of the Foreword. Mrs Marion Naifeh made the necessary arrangements for me to join the School for Advanced International Studies (SAIS) at Johns Hopkins University, Washington, DC, during the summer of 1988 as a visiting scholar. Indeed, the treatment I received from Dean Robert A. Lystad, Dean Packard and Dean Crowel was most touching and encouraging. The superb job done by Miss Teresa Simmons in handling and facilitating all my administrative work is also much appreciated.

Other close friends such as Mr Harry F. Kern, editor of the highly respected *Foreign Reports Bulletin* based in Washington, DC, his son Mr Nathaniel H. Kern, and Mr George A. Naifeh, former President of the American Arab Affairs Council, based in Washington, DC, were all supportive and highly encouraging. Special thanks and gratitude go to my efficient and WordPerfect expert Mrs Mary C. Schmidt and her husband Mr Michael Schmidt, who were very sincere in their support and help.

Academics such as Dr Bernard Reich and Dr Assad Homayoun at George Washington University, Professor Majid Khaddouri at SAIS and Professor R.K. Ramazani at the University of Virginia have all contributed significantly to the publishing of this work. Nor can I forget the late Professor Billy Winder from Princeton University who met me only two weeks before his demise, and offered me the extensive use of his rich personal library.

In Saudi Arabia, I was able to see and interview a number of Saudi diplomats and politicians who were kind enough to answer all my questions, make significant comments and extend their remarkable advice. In addition, Dr Muhammad Dorani from Qatar, an active member of the GCC headquarters in Riyadh, was always very supportive and an encouraging friend.

Acknowledgements

In Europe, I was granted an interview with Mr Nazir Famsah, who served as the representative of *Hayat* magazine in Iran and was Shah Muhammad Riza Pahlavi's adviser on Arab affairs. The interview was kindly arranged in Paris by the well-known Arab journalist Mr Samir Souki. In London I was privileged to be granted an interview with H.E. Ambassador Ja'far Ra'ed, who served as Iran's ambassador to the Kingdom of Saudi Arabia until April 1979. Ambassador Ra'ed, an outstanding diplomat, was always available for my questions. My thanks also go to H.E. Mr Amir Khosrow Afshar, Iran's acting Foreign Minister during the Shah's time, who was kind enough to see me in London and share his valuable thoughts with me, particularly regarding the Bahrain issue. Moreover, the assistance I received from Miss Virginia Forbes in London is much appreciated and valued.

To all these honourable people, dear friends and those who shared with me their knowledge, ideas and thoughts, I express my deep thanks and appreciation and hope sincerely that Almighty Allah will bless you all.

Riyadh, October 1992

Abbreviations and Acronyms

ARAMCO	Arabian American Oil Company
CASOC	California Arabian Standard Oil Company
CENTO	Central Treaty Organization
DLF	Dhufar Liberation Front
GCC	Gulf Co-operation Council
NIOC	National Iranian Oil Company
OIC	Organization of the Islamic Conference
OPEC	Organization of Petroleum Exporting Countries
PFLOAG	Popular Front for the Liberation of the Arabian Gulf
PLFO	Popular Front for the Liberation of Oman
SAMA	Saudi Arabian Monetary Agency
Socal	Standard Oil of California
TAPLINE	Trans-Arabian pipeline
UAE	United Arab Emirates
UAR	United Arab Republic
UN	United Nations
US	United States
USSR	Union of Soviet Socialist Republics

Glossary

adhan	Shi'a call for prayer
alim	Islamic scholar
amir	secular administrator
baraka	blessings
bay'ah	allegiance
fajr	morning prayer
fatwa	Islamic legal opinion
hajj	Grand Pilgrimage to Makkah
hajji	Muslim pilgrim
ibadah	worship
Ijma'	unanimity of opinion
mu'adhin	caller of Muslim prayer
mufti	Islamic legal expert
mujtahid	Islamic jurist and scholar
nizam	royal decree
qada'	Islamic courts
qadar	destiny
qadi	Islamic judge
salat	daily prayers
sawm	fasting of Ramadan
shahadah	Islamic creed
Shari'a	Islamic law
Sunna	teachings of the Prophet Muhammad
thob	robe
ulama	Islamic religious scholar
ummah	Islamic community
wali	governor
zakat	Islamic tax

Foreword

A common flaw of Western analysis of the non-Western world is the universal tendency to see one's subjects through one's own set of cultural, national and historical filters. This is particularly true of historical analysis of the Gulf, where Western interests and perceptions have dominated outsiders' views of internal political dynamics.

This assertion should not be construed as expressing the idea that internal Gulf political dynamics should dominate how Westerners see their interests there. It is up to each country, whether local or outside the region, to determine its own priority of foreign policy interests. The problem for outsiders arises when they begin to make the implicit assumption that their own political interests and priorities drive regional Gulf political dynamics, or that their priorities are even necessarily shared by Gulf political actors.

To gain a true understanding of Gulf political dynamics, one must view regional Gulf politics through the eyes of the local inhabitants. This little volume does just that. The author, a distinguished Saudi Arabian public servant and scholar, seeks, in examining Saudi–Iranian political, religious, economic and military relations, to contribute to a greater understanding of how the two countries related to each other over nearly 60 years, from 1925 to 1982 (the period 1925 to 1932 is introductory), how their approaches to domestic and regional politics were similar or differed, and how those differences and similarities contributed to the ongoing relationship.

It was not an easy book to write. During the early period under study, both countries were still in the process of political consolidation and transformation into modern states. During that time, much of the relationship was conducted informally so that very little in the way of written records exists. Outside powers, such as the United States and the United Kingdom, did keep extensive accounts of the region at the time, but their interests were focused on their own relations with the countries, not bilateral relations between the countries themselves.

Informal relations between the Arab and Persian sides of the Gulf are as old as history itself. By the mid-1920s, when the author begins his analysis, both Riza Shah of Iran and King Abd al-Aziz of what was to be Saudi Arabia were in the last stages of consolidating power and turning to the job of nation-building. As this process continued, the author compares the two countries' political systems, their politics and their approaches to foreign

Foreword

relations, including economic and military relations. He devotes a whole chapter to contrasting approaches to religion and religious relations between the two countries, a subject that most Western observers would probably choose to ignore.

The key contribution to note here is not so much the historical record that the author discusses, although that is important. Moreover, he introduces a number of fascinating subjects that are normally not covered in such studies, such as pre-World War attitudes towards the Gulf slave trade, an institution that bears little resemblance to the more commonly portrayed institution as it was practised in the West, particularly the United States. What is more valuable, however, in my opinion, is the rare insight into the perceptions of intra-Gulf politics as seen by one who is very representative of the Saudi Arabian government he so ably serves. As such, this is real history—not an interpretation by some outsider who looks first at the bare historical facts and then interprets them according to his or her own value system and political agenda, but a portrayal of the perceptions of a major actor, Saudi Arabia.

David E. Long
Burke, Virginia

Introduction

This book was supposed to be published over a year ago. But, like most others in the region, I was to become a victim of Saddam Hussein's invasion of Kuwait.

On 2 August 1990 I was in Washington, DC, trying to complete my research work and interviewing a number of scholars and senior political figures who had been recommended to me, when the invasion occurred and everything turned upside down. The whole world was stunned as a result of this aggression, and for a short while, the international community seemed paralysed. Children of all ages forgot the joys of summer as they became familiar with the name of Saddam Hussein. For men and women, in all walks of life, the Iraqi dictator became the main topic of conversation.

A month later, I decided to go back home to Saudi Arabia, hoping to do some writing. This was not to be. In Riyadh I found myself just as busy with other similar matters. On 17 January 1991 the war broke out and Saddam's SCUD missiles began falling on the Saudi capital as well as on the eastern parts of the country. There were moments when I thought of writing on the subject of the catastrophe that was taking place instead of the topic of Saudi–Iranian historical relations, which I had been researching. But I was saved by the volume of books, booklets and research papers that were published with amazing rapidity on the subject of Saddam Hussein himself, and on the history of the Iraqi–Kuwaiti border dispute.

Introduction

After the unexpectedly short war ended, I was able to return quickly to my PC and begin writing again. Later, in the summer of 1991, I went back to Washington, completed my research work for the remaining chapters and interviewed some of the people I had planned on seeing the summer before. Thank God, my book is now finished, and Kuwait has also been liberated.

The Kingdom of Saudi Arabia and Iran are two Middle Eastern countries which have always played a very important role in the political, economic and military life of the region. In the past, their geopolitical situation and economic disposition have always made them vital in any East–West calculations. Both World Wars underlined the strategic significance of the Red Sea and the Arabian/Persian Gulf to the warring parties. Thus any tilt towards either one of the competing sides by Iran or Saudi Arabia would have constituted a major advantage for the favoured side.

History has repeatedly shown the importance of the Kingdom of Saudi Arabia and Iran to the West. Their strategic location helped the Allied powers to win the Second World War by maintaining a monopoly of control in the so-called 'warm waters', while using the Gulf as their most assured way of getting badly needed supplies to the Russians on the Eastern Front.

With the discovery of oil, first in Iran and subsequently in Saudi Arabia, these countries have also become of major importance to the economies of the free world.

Due to a predicted fall in the future levels of oil production in the former Soviet Union, it is now generally assumed that the 1990s will witness an upsurge in demand by the former countries of the Eastern bloc (traditionally supplied by the USSR) for Gulf oil. Developments of this nature indicate that both Saudi Arabia and Iran, as well as other countries in the Gulf region, will remain a major international focal point for the foreseeable future.

This book, however, focuses solely on the bilateral relations between the Kingdom of Saudi Arabia and Iran from 1932 to 1982. The time-frame chosen for this study begins with the establishment of the Kingdom of Saudi Arabia as a fully sovereign, independent and unified country. However, due to the fact that the Pahlavi dynasty in Persia was established in 1925, the book also contains a chapter on pre-1932 relations, beginning in 1925.

Saudi Arabia in 1925 was known as the Kingdom of the Hijaz, Najd and its Dependencies. Its relations with Persia during the latter part of the 1920s and the early 1930s had their ups and downs. However, an enlightened policy of pragmatism led to the signing in 1929 of a Treaty of Friendship. This paved the way for constructive co-operation between the two countries until 1941, when Riza Shah Pahlavi (ruled 1925–41) was forced to abdicate in favour of his son, Muhammad Riza Shah Pahlavi (ruled 1941–79).

Introduction

The reasons encouraging me to carry out this work were many: first to highlight the importance of the Kingdom of Saudi Arabia and Iran to the free world; second, to examine and discuss the bilateral relations between Saudi Arabia and Iran from 1932 to 1982; third, to identify the political, economic and military priorities of the two countries; and finally, to analyse the impact and effects of the decision-making process in both Saudi Arabia and Iran. The primary objects of this book are covered in six chapters.

Chapter 1 deals with the historical background of Saudi–Persian relations from 1925 to 1932. In essence, this chapter sets the stage for understanding and identifying the issues of mutual concern, while providing an inside look at the short- and long-term strategies of both countries. The chapter also discusses how these two emerging nations became regionally influential and internationally important countries. The unification process carried out by King Abd al-Aziz in Saudi Arabia and by Riza Shah in Persia is also discussed.

Chapter 2 focuses on the political systems of the two countries. It also profiles their social and political entities, as well as their geopolitical structures. The primary objective is to identify, examine and compare similarities and differences between the two systems. The chapter also sheds some light on the type of monarchy adopted by each country.

Chapter 3 examines foreign policy and evaluates the bilateral political relations between Saudi Arabia and Iran from 1932 to 1982. Basically, it discusses the policy approaches of the two countries, showing that both were pursuing their own political goals in accordance with their perceived national interests. Concurrently, the chapter outlines the political priorities of Iran and Saudi Arabia, while also focusing on areas of co-operation and competition between them.

Chapter 4 focuses on the religious aspects of bilateral relations between Saudi Arabia and Iran, and discusses and evaluates the importance of Islam in both countries. The differences between Sunni and Shi'a Islam are also discussed. The chapter also deals with a number of important religious events which have contributed, both negatively and positively, to the overall bilateral religious relations between these two Islamic states.

Chapter 5 focuses on the economic aspects of Saudi–Iranian relations. It discusses and outlines the natural resources of the two countries. Furthermore, it examines the areas of co-operation and confrontation between them, as oil-producing nations, as well as the regional and international consequences of their actions. The importance to both countries of the Arabian/Persian Gulf, as a major international waterway, is also discussed and examined.

Introduction

Chapter 6 covers the sensitive topic of bilateral military relations and examines each country's military strategy, both for the Gulf region and for the Middle East as a whole. The 1979 Islamic revolution in Iran and some of its major consequences are also touched on. For the Kingdom of Saudi Arabia, the Islamic revolution was seen as an entirely domestic issue. For Iran and its new revolutionary leaders, however, it was seen as a commodity capable of being exported not only to neighbouring countries but to the Islamic world at large. As a result of such a vision, relations between the two countries began to deteriorate. This process was to be exacerbated after the outbreak of war between Iran and Iraq in 1980.

In summary, this book is about two fully independent, sovereign countries in the Middle East, which play a key role in the politics of the region. Both have in the past been allied to the West, while having chosen to maintain their individual identity by pursuing their own independent policies. The present analysis attempts to provide answers regarding likely courses of action that might be pursued by the two countries *vis-à-vis* their bilateral relations in the future.

1
Historical Background 1925–32

In 1925 Abd al-Aziz ibn Abd al-Rahman Al Saud, known to the West as Ibn Saud, was still engaged in reunifying what is now the Kingdom of Saudi Arabia. Abd al-Aziz (ruled 1902–53) was a giant of a man, both physically and as a leader. Well over six feet tall, his imposing figure was matched by a charismatic personality. At the same time, he was patient and pragmatic in his dealings, not only with his people but also with foreign countries, particularly the Great Powers of his time. Consequently, he was considered an outstanding leader among his people and an outstanding diplomat among the Arabs.[1]

The unification process had begun in 1902, when Abd al-Aziz's father, Abd al-Rahman, named him Amir of Najd, or Central Arabia, and Imam of the followers of a puritanical Islamic revival movement founded in the mid-eighteenth century by Muhammad ibn Abd al-Wahhab.[2] Abd al-Aziz immediately set out to regain Saudi political control in the Arabian peninsula, which had been lost to the Al Rashids of Ha'il in the late nineteenth century, and to spread the Islamic revival movement which the House of Saud had championed since Abd al-Wahhab's day.[3]

Following the capture of Ha'il in 1921, Abd al-Aziz elevated Najd from an emirate to a sultanate and took the title Sultan of Najd and its Dependencies. In 1926 he captured the Kingdom of Hijaz on the Red Sea coast, including the holy cities of Makkah and Madinah. Originally, Najd and Hijaz were joined only under the personal rule of Abd al-Aziz, who became King of the Hijaz.[4] Slowly, however, a single country began to emerge. Known as the Kingdom of the Hijaz, Najd and its Dependencies until the acquisition of the province of Asir, south of the Hijaz, in 1931, the country was renamed the Kingdom of Saudi Arabia by Abd al-Aziz in 1932.[5]

Persia (the country was renamed Iran in 1935) was also undergoing a period of political rejuvenation in 1925. Riza Pahlavi, the father of the last Shah, Muhammad Riza, had seized power in 1921 as Riza Khan after a bloodless *coup d'état*. An ardent nationalist, he had risen through the ranks as a military man and did not know how to read or write.[6] Riza Khan was a great admirer of Kemal Ataturk and his efforts to create a modern secular state from the ruins of the old Ottoman Empire. As a nationalist, Riza also wanted to abolish the monarchical system of government in Persia, but, ironically in light of the creation of the Islamic Republic in 1979, he backed down in the face of strong opposition from the Shi'a Islamic religious establishment.[7] In 1925 Riza Khan deposed the Qajar dynasty and in the following year had himself crowned Riza Shah Pahlavi. He nevertheless believed that the Islam espoused by the Shi'a clergy was backward, and throughout his reign he strove to create a secular nationalistic society.[8]

In the 1930s Riza Shah sought to neutralize British and French influence in Persia by strengthening political ties with Nazi Germany and supporting many of its foreign policy positions.[9] His machinations with the Germans ultimately cost him his throne: in 1941 the British forced him to abdicate in favour of his son, Muhammad Riza Shah Pahlavi.

An important factor in the political relations between Persia and Saudi Arabia during this period was the similarity of the stages in their political development—both countries were undergoing the process of nation-building. This process in what was to become Saudi Arabia began after the total capture of the Hijaz by Saudi forces in 1926. Prior to that time, the Saudi state had been confined to Najd (Central Arabia), an area where there was very little foreign influence. Politics were organized along tribal lines and *Shari'a* (Islamic law), supplemented by unwritten tribal law, was the law of the land. The Sultanate of Najd and its Dependencies did not require a complex system of administration, and Sultan Abd al-Aziz was able to run the affairs of state through a number of trusted aides and counsellors.

With the conquest of the Hijaz, the newly established King faced a new political situation. The Hijaz had its own cabinet form of government and judicial system which were far more sophisticated than the personalized system of public administration in Najd. The King also had to deal with a third system of law, the Turkish code, which had been used in the Hijaz since the days of Ottoman rule. In addition, he acquired the public administration of the *hajj*, or Grand Pilgrimage to Makkah. Pilgrims from every corner of the Islamic world came annually to perform their religious duties and, indeed, the *hajj* was a major source of foreign exchange for the Hijaz. Abd al-Aziz was determined to make the *hajj* a model of administration for the entire Muslim world, making sure that the pilgrims were treated fairly by the pilgrim guides and merchants who formed a complex service industry. To cope with these new conditions, King Abd al-Aziz promulgated an Organic Law for the Hijaz on 29 August 1926. Subsequently, on 29 January 1927, the Hijaz was incorporated with Najd into the Kingdom of the Hijaz, Najd and its Dependencies.

The next step in the King's efforts to unify Saudi Arabia was to conquer the principality of Asir in the south-western part of the peninsula. In 1931 Abd al-Aziz advanced on Asir, including the two cities of Najran and Jizan. He based his move on a 1926 agreement between himself and the ruler of Asir, al-Idrisi, under which Asir came under Saudi protection.[10] In 1931 al-Idrisi repudiated the agreement and King Abd al-Aziz responded by incorporating Asir as a Saudi province. On 23 September 1932 he issued a Royal Decree (2716) renaming the country the Kingdom of Saudi Arabia.

The reunification process under Riza Pahlavi occurred along somewhat different lines. The first internal challenge he had to face was the nature of the political system itself. In March 1924 there had been a serious parliamentary debate about the country's constitution as well as the nature of the political system. Sentiment for changing the monarchy into a republic was growing, despite the opposition of the religious leaders, who feared that Islam would face the same fate in Iran that it had encountered in Turkey under Ataturk.[11]

Riza Pahlavi took advantage of this issue to strengthen his position and impose his wishes on parliament, particularly after theatening to advance with his army against Tehran.[12] He was then able to turn his attention to another issue, the re-annexation by Persia of Khuzistan. At the time, a local Arab ruler, Sheikh Khaz'al, was seeking recognition of an independent state of Arabistan, the name used by the region's predominantly Arab-speaking population as well as by neighbouring Arab states.[13] From Riza Khan's perspective, the area was historically a part of Persia and the British were conspiring to separate it from Persia and thus gain control of its oil resources. Taking advantage of the political turmoil that rocked the area, Riza Khan sent in troops: Arabistan was conquered on 20 April 1925. Following this victory, Riza Shah continued to consolidate his power; on 1 October 1925 he deposed the last Qajar Shah, who went into exile in Paris, and appointed himself the new Shah of Persia.[14] He was crowned as the first Shah of the Pahlavi dynasty in 1926.

The occupation of Arabistan by Riza Pahlavi in 1925 had not gone unnoticed by Abd al-Aziz, but he was engaged in the process of unifying the Arabian peninsula and was, in any event, in no position to contest it. Nevertheless, the annexation of Arabistan led the King to become very much aware of Riza Shah's ambitions in the Gulf region, particularly with respect to Bahrain. The Persians had long claimed sovereignty over Bahrain, which has a large Shi'a population. Thus on 20 May 1927 King Abd al-Aziz signed a bilateral treaty with the British in Jeddah in which he recognized the governments of Bahrain, Kuwait, Qatar and Oman and their special treaties with Britain.[15]

Persia considered the 1927 British–Saudi treaty a direct challenge to its sovereignty over Bahrain. In response, Riza Shah ordered his envoy in Cairo to submit a 'memorandum of objection' to the Saudi government and demand the return of Bahrain to Persian domain and authority.[16] On 26 November 1927 Persia lodged an official complaint with the League of Nations.[17] This territorial dispute over Bahrain remained unresolved until 1968, when King Faisal of Saudi Arabia and Muhammad Riza Shah met in Jeddah to work out a peaceful settlement which came about under United Nations auspices.

In summary, the political dimension of Saudi–Persian relations during the second half of the 1920s was characterized by a number of similarities and contradictions. Both countries were experiencing similar processes of political consolidation, but their bilateral relations were marked by both friendship (in the form of the 1929 treaty) and rivalry (particularly over Riza Pahlavi's territorial ambitions in the Gulf). King Abd al-Aziz, on the other hand, was more interested in consolidating his country than expanding his political boundaries.[18] Moreover, the Saudi monarch saw the value of maintaining good relations with the Great Powers, whereas Riza Shah Pahlavi tried to play one off against the other to Persia's benefit. As previously mentioned, this policy ultimately cost him his throne when the British ousted him in 1941 because of his close relations with Nazi Germany.

The Security Dimension

National security, both internal and external, is an important, if not the most vital, factor in any country's stability. Thus both King Abd al-Aziz and Riza Shah paid a great deal of attention to their respective national security policies. However, each monarch approached it from his own perspective and pursued a different policy.

Historical Background 1925-32

Internal Security
Saudi Arabia and Iran both have traditional, tribal-oriented societies. The relationship between the state and the tribes, therefore, was particularly important during the state-building process. Tribalism was viewed by both leaders as a potential internal security problem.

Sultan Abd al-Aziz's approach to tribalism was unique: by incorporating it into his system of government, he made it a source of internal stability rather than a threat. First, he continued to encourage the spread of the Wahhabi revival movement among the tribes. Second, and closely associated with the first point, he began sending religious teachers to educate the various tribes in accordance with the principal teachings of Islam. Third, he created a bedouin army, the Ikhwan (Brethren) both to spread the revival and to unite the country. Fourth, to secure the political loyalty of the important tribal chiefs and sheikhs, he entered into marital relationships with their daughters, as well as their sisters.[19] Fifth, he adopted a plan of settling the tribes in agricultural areas. And, sixth, he practised generosity as a means of winning the hearts and minds of the tribal leaders.

All these efforts were greatly aided by Abd al-Aziz's charismatic personality and generous nature. The following story illustrates his generosity:

> When the Packard sedan in which Abd al-Aziz Ibn Saud, King of Saudi Arabia, was making his pilgrimage to Mecca [Makkah] blew out a tire, His Majesty got out and sat down in the sand to wait while it was being fixed. While he was waiting, a shepherd on a camel rode up and, unaware to whom he was speaking, asked whether the King had gone by. Ibn Saud replied that the King had not passed yet but was expected to do so soon and asked why the shepherd wanted to know. 'I heard that he was on his way to Mecca and want to see if he will give me some money so I can make the pilgrimage too,' replied the shepherd, dismounting.[20]

The story goes on and on; after more than fifteen minutes of chatting with the shepherd, the King hands him a fistful of money which is more than enough for his pilgrimage trip. This kind of impulsive, generous nature was well known to his people, winning him the loyalty of the tribes and enabling him further to consolidate his power in the major parts of the Arabian peninsula.

Abd al-Aziz was also aided in his quest for internal security, particularly in newly conquered regions, by a highly practical decision-making style and a penchant for prompt action. For example, when the Hijaz came fully under his sovereignty in 1926, the King preserved the customs and traditions of the region, a step that won him the loyalty of the Hijazis. Moreover, his efforts to make the annual *hajj* as safe and efficient as possible enhanced his internal popularity and won him respect throughout the Muslim world.[21] At the same time, he did not hesitate to meet security problems head on when the need arose. In 1929 he moved decisively against a group of disgruntled tribesmen from the Ikhwan who had grown restive when there were no more battles to fight: the King defeated them at Sibilla in what was to be the last great bedouin battle. In short, Abd al-Aziz's wise and judicious approach to internal security went far towards overcoming centuries-old tribal animosities and regional rivalries and enabled him to maintain a high order of stability in his newly formed kingdom.

Riza Shah Pahlavi took a very different approach to tribalism. He saw tribal societies as incompatible with national unity and a menace to internal security.[22] This view led him to seek to demolish the social, economic and political structure of Persian tribal society.[23] His de-tribalization policies were very harsh. He executed tribal leaders and placed tribal territories under the jurisdiction of the army and later under the gendarmerie. His maltreatment of the nomadic tribes is considered by some historians as one of the most sordid chapters of his reign.[24]

Although he worked hard to modernize and centralize the public administration, Riza Shah was no democrat, believing that democratic institutions could not work in Persian society.[25] He was an ardent nationalist, however, and resented British encroachments on Persian sovereignty. This is one reason why he aligned himself with Nazi Germany. He also allowed Persian nationalists at home great political power.[26] In his attempt to create a new social order in his country, Riza Shah forced through many drastic and far-reaching changes, frequently using force to implement them. This often meant brutal actions by the army in various Persian provinces, and a tolerance of repressive army measures against opposition forces.[27] These measures, together with the judicious use of oil revenues, were applied to control his ministers, the bureaucracy, the parliament, the public and the media, thus enabling Riza Shah to maintain internal security more through fear and greed than popularity.

Despite their different approaches, both Abd al-Aziz and Riza Pahlavi were able to maintain a fair degree of internal stability in their fledgling regimes. The stability of the Saudi regime proved the more lasting, however, as it was based on religious conviction, loyalty to a charismatic leader and tribal identity. Riza Pahlavi's regime was never popular.

Historical Background 1925-32

External Security
In the years 1925-32 regional Gulf security was not the great international issue it had been during the First World War or was to become during the Second World War and up to the present day. Most external security threats were local and concerned territorial disputes over the many non-demarcated borders. The demarcation of borders became important with the discovery of oil along international frontiers and in the Gulf, but this was still largely in the future. Britain, the predominant Great Power in the region, used its influence on the side of the states under British mandate or British protection, but rarely were any other outside powers involved.

Historically, territorial boundaries had not been of particular importance. Large areas were uninhabited except for sporadic visits by nomadic tribes, and sovereignty was largely determined by tribal allegiances and by a leader's ability to subjugate the lands on the periphery of his domain. Since, over millennia, domains had expanded and contracted, appeared and disappeared, virtually any leader could look to some point of maximum territorial control in his people's historic past and claim that this was his country's rightful domain. As his neighbour could do likewise, there were inevitable territorial disputes until the long and often painful process of delineating borders was completed. In the 1920s both Abd al-Aziz and Riza Shah were confronted with multiple such disputes.

At that time, the Saudis had virtually no demarcated boundaries and initially saw little need for them. The British were pressing for boundaries in the north, however, and there were conflicting territorial claims elsewhere, based largely on tribal allegiances and historical conquests. The following are among the more pressing territorial disputes facing Abd al-Aziz in the 1920s and early 1930s.

Saudi-Kuwaiti-Iraqi Borders. The British were concerned at Abd al-Aziz's taking control of Wadi Sirhan on the Najdi frontier with Transjordan and Iraq and at raids by Abd al-Aziz's Ikhwan warriors, and invited Abd al-Aziz to participate in talks to demarcate the Najdi Sultanate's border with Iraq and Kuwait. The Saudi delegation negotiated the Treaty of Muhammara in May 1922.

In drawing the border line, the treaty assigned various tribes along the frontier to the rulers of the three states. Abd al-Aziz demurred, however, saying that the Saudi delegation had exceeded its powers and that some of the tribes loyal to him had been placed under Iraqi sovereignty. He requested a personal meeting with Sir Percy Cox, the British High Commissioner in Baghdad, to iron out the differences. They met in November 1922 at Uqayr, a Saudi village on the Gulf coast, where they signed another agreement by which Najdi and Iraqi tribes were allowed equal rights and free access to wells and grazing along an unfortified frontier; a neutral zone was to be created between the two countries similar to that created between Najd and Kuwait.

The Najdi-Kuwaiti neutral zone included 2,000 square miles (5,000 sq. km). It was abolished in the 1960s and the territory was divided equally between Saudi Arabia and Kuwait. Since oil production and the exploitation of other mineral resources in the area could not be so divided, it was agreed that the two countries should share the revenues equally.[28] The Najdi-Iraqi neutral zone covered 2,500 square miles (6,500 sq. km). In 1938 the Saudi and Iraqi governments further defined relations dealing with the neutral zone, and in 1975 the two countries reached a final agreement fixing their mutual borders.[29]

Despite the demarcation of the northern Najdi borders, Ikhwan warriors under tribal leaders such as Faisal al-Dawish continued to cloud the security issue with cross-border raids into Kuwait and Iraq. This situation continued until they were finally subdued by Abd al-Aziz at the Battle of Sibilla in 1929.

The Saudi-Bahraini Water Rights Issue. This issue developed early in the 1930s when Saudi Arabia and Bahrain claimed sovereignty over three tiny islands in the Gulf: Abu Saafa, Greater Lebinah and Lesser Lebinah. Consequently, the two countries engaged in talks and negotiations which continued until the 1960s, when the two states were able to agree to the following terms: (a) Abu Saafa would be under Saudi sovereignty and oil revenues from the island would be shared by both countries; (b) Saudi Arabia would have full sovereignty over Greater Lebinah; and (c) Bahrain would have full sovereignty over Lesser Lebinah.[30]

The Buraimi Oasis Issue. This issue involved conflicting claims over an oasis known as al-Buraimi, located in a triangle where Saudi Arabia, Abu Dhabi and the Sultanate of Oman meet.[31] All three countries claimed the oasis. Abu Dhabi and Oman claimed ancient tribal ties; the Saudi claim extended back to the nineteenth century when the local tribes adopted the teachings of the Wahhabi revival and gave their allegiance to the Al Sauds. The issue was addressed by King Abd al-Aziz in 1933 when he asked the British, who had a protective status in both Oman and Abu Dhabi, to recognize his demand to demarcate the eastern borders of the Kingdom. Negotiations began but bore no fruit, and the issue was put before the United Nations in the 1950s.

A dramatic, positive change took place following Britain's announcement in 1968 of its intention to withdraw from the Gulf region by 1971. In 1971

Historical Background 1925–32

the Saudis agreed to recognize Omani sovereignty over three of the nine villages of al-Buraimi and Abu Dhabi sovereignty over the other six. Saudi Arabia and Abu Dhabi signed an agreement on 29 July 1974 under which oil revenues from that area were to be shared by the two states; Saudi Arabia was to be granted access to the Gulf across Abu Dhabi, through Khawr al-Udayd.[32] The main reason behind the Saudi decision was the desire to strengthen the newly created United Arab Emirates (UAE) and foster unity among the emirates which had joined the federation. Saudi Arabia strongly believed in the necessity of the union for the stability of the small emirates (formerly the Trucial States) which had received independence from Britain in 1971.

The Saudi–Yemeni Border Issue. The border disputes between King Abd al-Aziz and the Imam of Yemen began in 1931 when the two countries shared a common western frontier following Abd al-Aziz's capture of the province of Asir and its two principal cities, Najran and Jizan.[33] Relations worsened and led to the invasion of Yemen by Saudi forces in 1934. Peace talks resulted in the Treaty of Taif in May of that year. The treaty included a Pact of Arbitration, valid for 20 years, and was subject to prolongation or abrogation upon either party's giving notice 6 months prior to the end of the 20-year pact. The treaty and its associated pact continue to be the most important document defining Saudi–Yemeni boundaries today.

Saudi borders with the south of Yemen remain undemarcated. This was never a real problem during the period of British occupation. After South Yemen became an independent state in 1967 there were occasional border flare-ups, although the borders are currently quiet.

Today the borders of Saudi Arabia are virtually all demarcated or at least not actively contested. As we have seen, however, this was not the case in the years 1925–32. Thus, establishing secure borders was a major preoccupation of Abd al-Aziz both then and in succeeding years in his dealings with Persia/Iran.

Riza Pahlavi was also confronted with a number of territorial disputes, many of which were not resolved until years later. Like Abd al-Aziz, he placed a high priority on settling his border disputes with neighbouring countries in order to achieve external security and internal stability. The following were among the most pressing territorial disputes.

Iran–Iraq Boundaries. Iran and Iraq share a common border for some 550 miles (885 km) and territorial disputes along it go back many years. Perhaps the most acrimonious dispute in recent years has been over where to draw the boundary down the Shatt al-Arab. The Shatt is formed by the confluence of the Tigris and Euphrates rivers and forms a common border between Iraq and Iran for much of its course.[34] In strategic and commercial terms, it is probably more important to Iraq because the Iraqi Gulf coast is very small whereas Iran extends for the entire eastern shore of the Gulf.

The Shatt al-Arab problem goes back to 1847, when the Ottomans and Persians signed the Erzurum Treaty. According to the treaty, the Ottomans recognized Persian sovereignty over the largely Arab city of Muhammara in what is now Khuzistan; the Persians, in return, recognized Ottoman sovereignty over the Shatt al-Arab to the high-water mark on the Persian side, allowing Persian-bound vessels free navigation in the Shatt.[35] In 1913 the Ottomans and Persians signed a protocol, under British and Russian mediation, which followed the same basic formula with Ottoman sovereignty over the river and its islands. However, Persian sovereignty extended out to the middle of the river in two strips, one adjacent to Muhammara (known today as Khorramshahr) and the other adjacent to the city of Abadan. The border remained thus until the collapse of Ottoman rule in Iraq after the First World War, leading to the creation of Iraq as a British mandate and the rise of Riza Pahlavi in Persia in 1925. Riza claimed Persian sovereignty to the middle of the river.

Over time, the Shatt al-Arab issue has been a major irritant in Iranian relations with Iraq, and has thus had an impact on its relations with all Arab Gulf states including Saudi Arabia. In 1934 an independent Iraq brought the issue of the Shatt before the League of Nations, accusing Persia of breaking all treaties legitimizing Iraqi rights to the river.[36] Iraq conceded Iranian sovereignty in a mediated settlement known as the Algiers Agreement in 1975, but the problem was to resurface when the Iran–Iraq war broke out in the 1980s.

The Kurdish Problem. Another often acrimonious territorial issue affecting Iranian–Iraqi as well as Iranian–Turkish relations concerns the Kurds, a separate ethnic group that inhabits parts of Iran, Iraq and Turkey. The Kurds have long sought an independent Kurdish state but have been too internally divided to work together towards that end. This has produced both internal and external problems for Iran and Iraq as renegade Kurdish tribesmen have sought safe havens on both sides of the border. During the 1920s, and indeed up to the Iraqi revolution of 1958, the two countries honoured the 1913 Ottoman–Persian protocol and neither used the Kurdish situation against the other. Iraq's relations with Iran, never cordial, then began to deteriorate. Since then, both countries have used the Kurds as political leverage against the other. This was particularly true of Iran, which used the

Historical Background 1925-32

Kurdish issue as leverage in seeking to force Iraq to recognize Iranian sovereignty to the middle of the Shatt al-Arab.[37]

The Kurdish problem was also the most contentious issue in Riza Pahlavi's relations with Turkey during the first few years of his reign. Nomadic Kurdish tribes crossed the 282-mile (454-km) Turkish-Persian frontier as freely as they crossed the Iraqi-Persian frontier. Moreover, many Persian Kurds allied themselves with the communist movement in Persia, later known as the Tudeh Party, a tie that was anathema to the Turks. Strains over the Kurdish issue were finally resolved when Riza Shah visited Turkey in June 1934, initiating a new era in Persian-Turkish relations.[38] Although the Kurdish minorities in Iran, Turkey and Iraq are still active and demand full autonomy over their territories, they have not been able to achieve their goal. There are estimated to be 2 million Kurds in Iraq, 4-5 million in Turkey, 3 million in Iran, approximately 300,000 in Syria and some 175,000 in the ex-Soviet Union.[39]

Persian-Soviet Borders. The history of Russian-Persian border relations is a complicated issue. The Persians have traditionally viewed their northern neighbours with distrust, due to their fear of Russia's southward expansionism, military aggressiveness and political interference.[40] After the Second World War, it was US pressure which forced the evacuation of Soviet troops from northern Iran in 1946. Earlier, in 1920, Red Army contingents entered Persia's Caspian region, seeking to help a local rebel, Kuchek Khan, establish a 'Soviet Republic of Gilan'.[41] This puppet republic fell in 1922, when Riza Khan came to power and the Red Army withdrew from northern Persian territories.

A Soviet-Persian Treaty of Friendship signed on 26 February 1921 granted the Soviets 'the right to advance [their] troops into the Persian interior' if a third party 'should desire to use Persian territory as a base of operations against Russia'.[42] The treaty secured peaceful relations between the two countries for a quarter of a century: throughout the reign of Riza Shah, the Iranian-Soviet border remained undisturbed.

Persian-Afghan Borders. Iran and Afghanistan share a common border of 528 miles (850 km). Relations between the two countries today are relatively calm, but in the early years of Riza Pahlavi's reign this was not so. In 1929 Riza Shah sent officers and advisers to assist King Amanullah Khan of Afghanistan against a potential revolt by Muslim clerics and Pushtun tribesmen who resented the King's decree adopting Western reforms.[43] This action antagonized the Afghan tribes residing near the Persian-Afghan border who initiated a series of cross-border raids. In response, Riza Shah demanded that King Amanullah cede Afghanistan's western Herat province to Persia.[44] When the King rejected the demand outright, Riza Shah deployed a heavily armed force near the Afghan frontier. He was dissuaded from taking direct military action against Afghanistan, however, by the hostile reaction of Russia and Turkey.[45] The crisis was resolved when King Amanullah abdicated and a new Afghan government was installed. Riza Shah not only refrained from further interference in the internal affairs of Afghanistan, but even opened his country's doors to many Afghan refugees, as well as to members of the former ruling family.

Persia's Claim to Bahrain. The Persian claim to Bahrain extends back for centuries and was renewed by Riza Pahlavi when he came to power. Thus, when the Saudi-British treaty was signed in Jeddah on 20 May 1927 whereby King Abd al-Aziz agreed to establish friendly, peaceful relations with Bahrain, Kuwait, Qatar and Oman,[46] Riza Shah objected on the grounds that it was a provocative rejection of Persia's claim to Bahrain. He thereupon submitted a petition to the League of Nations demanding the restoration of Persian sovereignty over the island. The territorial dispute was not settled until Bahrain gained its independence in 1971. In any event, the issue constituted a greater threat to the security of Bahrain than to that of Iran.

Persian Claims to Islands in the Lower Gulf. Riza Pahlavi also revived Persian claims to a number of islands in the lower Gulf, notably the Tunbs and Abu Musa which belonged to two small sheikhdoms belonging to the Trucial States (now the UAE). Having understood the strategic and economic importance of the Strait of Hormuz, Riza Shah aimed to control as much of the waterway as possible. (In addition, red oxide had been discovered in commercial quantities on Abu Musa.) In 1925 the Shah began to build a naval fleet which could challenge British naval domination of the Gulf region. By 1927 Persia's naval power represented a real threat to many of the Gulf islands. In May 1928 Persian naval forces occupied the island of Hinjam and began to antagonize the inhabitants of many other islands.[47] The years from 1929 to 1939 witnessed extensive but unsuccessful talks and negotiations between Iran and Britain over the sovereignty of these islands, particularly Abu Musa and the Greater and Lesser Tunbs. Negotiations were suspended with the outbreak of the Second World War, and although the British acceded to Iranian claims to the three islands in 1971, the Arab sheikhdoms have not accepted the loss of their territory.

As the foregoing has shown, although the unification process and nation-building techniques in Saudi Arabia and Persia began in very similar political

Historical Background 1925-32

circumstances, there were some major differences (see Table 1). Riza Shah attempted to create a modern nation from the top down whereas Abd al-Aziz instituted changes on a solid base of religious and political tradition. In the long run, his method proved more durable.

It was during the early years of transition for both countries, 1925-32, that modern Saudi-Iranian relations began to take shape. Bilateral relations essentially had the following major dimensions: religious, political and security.

The Religious Dimension

Religion has been and will remain an important factor in Saudi relations with all Muslim countries, including Iran, for two reasons. First, the rise of the Al Saud dynasty from rulers of a small Najdi township to rulers of a modern oil kingdom coincided with its championing of the Islamic revival of Muhammad ibn Abd al-Wahhab. In no other modern Muslim country has Islam permeated the political system for such a long period as in Saudi Arabia. Moreover, the creation of an Islamic Republic in Iran in 1979 has served only to intensify the Islamic dimension of relations between the two countries. Second, Saudi Arabia is geographically the 'heartland of Islam'. It contains the two holy cities of Makkah and Madinah where Islam was born, where it matured under the Prophet Muhammad (Peace be upon him), and where the holy Quran was revealed. Makkah is the holiest site in Islam, with Islam's central holy shrine, the Ka'bah, whereas Madinah contains the tomb of the Prophet Muhammad and his mosque.

When King Abd al-Aziz captured Makkah in 1924 and Madinah in 1926, he aroused the concern of a number of Muslim countries including Persia. The key issues were the future of the two holy places and allegations that the Saudis, during their capture of the holy cities, had seriously damaged the holy shrines. Many Muslim countries feared that Abd al-Aziz and his zealous Ikhwan warriors would restrict access to the holy places to those who espoused the fundamentalist doctrines of their religious revival. They also feared that many sites had been damaged in the fighting to take the two holy cities.

King Abd al-Aziz refuted all these allegations and declared that he fully welcomed an investigation of the holy places by any Muslim state.[48] His declaration was particularly aimed at King Fouad of Egypt, who objected to King Abd al-Aziz's acquisition of the Hijaz and its holy cities. (King Fouad had ambitions to establish Cairo as the capital of Islam and himself as the Caliph of Islam.[49]) Unlike King Fouad or King Hussein, the ex-King of the

Table 1. Saudi Arabia and Iran: a Comparative Chart of Means and Methods during the Early Stages of Nation-building

Processes	Means and methods of King Abd al-Aziz of Saudi Arabia	Means and methods of Riza Shah of Iran
Unification process	Limited use of force (force as an end), alliances, treaties, and convincing ways	Unlimited use of force (force as a means), oppressive and suppressive measures, and annexation of non-Persian territories (Arabistan)
Nation-building	Earning loyalty through generosity, settlement of bedouin, guarantee of rights, implementation of *Shari'a* law, respect of *ulama* and charismatic leadership	Absolute rule, suppression of minorities and political parties, and condemnation of clergy
Internal policy	Limited modernization without disruption of tradition and customs, build-up of regular army, adoption of *shura* system, and sharing rule with sons and loyalists	Full modernization along European lines, disruption of traditions and customs, liberation of women, political manoeuvring, strengthening of army, creation of a puppet parliament and focus on communications
External policy	Limited ambitions, pro-British and Western policy, condemnation of communism and zionism, friendly ties and treaties with neighbouring states	Unlimited ambitions, anti-British policy, alliance with Nazi Germany, and anti-communist stance

Historical Background 1925-32

Hijaz, who, prior to his downfall in 1926, had proclaimed himself 'King of Arab Kings' and also had pretensions to be Caliph, Abd al-Aziz made no claims to political or religious leadership of the entire Islamic world. He acknowledged that Makkah and Madinah were important to all Muslims and proclaimed that the Islamic community would have the right to determine the administration of the holy places.[50]

Riza Pahlavi, the first Muslim leader to respond to Abd al-Aziz's offer, sent delegations to both Makkah and Madinah to investigate the allegations of damage. Given the generally anti-religious nature of his regime, however, his concern for the Muslim holy places appears to have been based more on political than on religious motives. At home, he considered the religious establishment as an opponent. This led him to suppress the clergy, deprive them of many of their traditional privileges, and seek to undermine their influence with the people.[51]

The first Persian delegation arrived in Jeddah on 21 October 1925 to investigate the situation in Makkah. It consisted of Mirza Ali Akbar Khan Buhman, Persia's Minister to Egypt, and Habibollah Khan Hoveida, Persia's Consul-General in Palestine.[52] In addition to investigating the situation in Makkah, the delegation was assigned the task of making arrangements for a second delegation to visit Madinah.

Prior to the investigation, Riza Shah's government had already accepted as accurate reports that King Abd al-Aziz's followers had damaged the holy places.[53] It had also published an official announcement condemning the Saudis in exceedingly strong terms.[54] However, this did not deter King Abd al-Aziz from receiving the Persian delegation and facilitating its mission. His reception of the delegation was described as cordial, and he provided it with his own automobiles to journey on to Makkah.[55] In his talks with the Persians, the King repeated his position of welcoming a delegation from any other Muslim country to investigate the alleged charges.

After completing its mission in Makkah, the delegation returned to Jeddah, which was still under siege by the Saudi forces. Despite the fact that the delegation did not communicate further with King Abd al-Aziz, its members concluded that Makkah under the Saudis was in a much better condition than it had been during the time of the Hashimites.[56]

The second delegation, sent to investigate the situation in Madinah and led by Persia's Consul to Damascus, arrived in Jeddah on 20 October 1925. In his book, *An Arabian Diary*, Sir Gilbert Clayton describes the delegation setting out for Madinah:

> The Persian Consul from Damascus left about 4:30 p.m. in a Ford car for Mecca [Makkah] on his wearisome trip to Medina [Madinah], looking

very dejected and unhappy and accompanied by an even more miserable looking orderly in the garb of a Persian policeman but wearing white sand shoes.[57]

From Clayton's description, the members of the second delegation appear to have been more critical of the Saudis and more prone to accept allegations of damage to the holy places than the first delegation. Although no comments were made by the Persians to the Saudi officials upon their return from Madinah, the general feeling was that the delegation was particularly unhappy at the Saudis' destruction of some venerated domed tombs there.

Abd al-Aziz had indeed destroyed some tombs in Madinah as well as the so-called tomb of Eve in Jeddah which many Muslims visited during the *hajj*. The destruction of such tombs had nothing to do with the Saudi capture of the Hijaz, however. It had become common practice in the Islamic world for famous holy men to be buried in domed mausoleums, and for people to make pilgrimages to them for *baraka* (blessings). The Saudis strongly believed that the veneration of the tombs of saints and holy men was a desecration of the worship of God and God alone. This precept was a major teaching of Muhammad ibn Abd al-Wahhab, and to this day, even Saudi kings are buried in unmarked graves to prevent their burial sites from becoming objects of religious veneration. Iranians, on the other hand, have long recognized Shi'a Islam as the state religion. This branch of Islam contains far more elements of mysticism than Sunni Islam, which is practised by most of the world's 800 million Muslims, and particularly the conservative Hanbali school of Sunni Islamic jurisprudence embraced by Muhammad ibn Abd al-Wahhab and followed by the vast majority of Saudis.[58]

Abd al-Aziz was keen to maintain good relations with all the leaders of the Islamic world regardless of the religious policies in their respective countries. Further, he disregarded the sectarian religious differences among the Muslim *ummah* (community). His concern was to unify the position of the Muslim *ummah* and safeguard the Islamic holy places. Consequently, he called for an Islamic Conference to be held in Makkah and to be attended by all Muslim leaders.[59] The conference took place in Makkah during the *hajj* season of 1926. Thus, despite the differences in Islamic doctrine between Saudi Arabia and Persia, Abd al-Aziz's invitation to Persia to attend the conference was accepted. Only Egypt, under the leadership of King Fouad, declined to attend. The success of the conference enabled Abd al-Aziz to establish and continue to improve Saudi relations with other Muslim nations, with the exception of Egypt under King Fouad. Relations with Persia, in particular, continued to improve. For example, during the 1928 *hajj* season,

Historical Background 1925-32

Persian pilgrims to Makkah and Madinah totalled 3,403, a relatively large number for the time.[60]

The Political Dimension

The first formal diplomatic intercourse between Persia and what was then the Sultanate of Najd occurred in 1925 when Persia tried to mediate between Abd al-Aziz and King Ali of the Hijaz during the Saudi siege of Jeddah.[61] Abd al-Aziz accepted the mediation offer, but insisted that Ali join his father, ex-King Hussein, in exile. While civil order was improving in Makkah under the Al Sauds, civil order in Jeddah was slowly deteriorating. Consequently, the city fell to Abd al-Aziz in December 1925; two weeks later, in 1926, the Saudi forces captured Madinah. Thus, although the Persian mediation effort was stillborn, it constituted a major step towards establishing political relations between the two countries.

In 1927 Habibollah Khan Hoveida became the first Persian diplomat to visit the Kingdom of the Hijaz, Najd and its Dependencies. He conducted diplomatic talks with Saudi officials with the aim of establishing diplomatic relations between the two countries.[62]

The high point in Saudi–Persian political relations during the second half of the 1920s was the Friendship Treaty of 1929, signed in Tehran on 24 August of that year.[63] The treaty was concluded by the Persians and a three-man Saudi delegation led by Sheikh Abdallah al-Fadl, the Supervisor of Foreign Affairs, who was authorized by King Abd al-Aziz to sign on his behalf. The delegation arrived in Tehran on 10 August;[64] two days later, it was received by Riza Shah, who awarded its members Persian decorations.[65] Following the signing of the treaty on 24 August, they made their way back to Jeddah by way of Baghdad.

In essence, the Friendship Treaty set out the basic principles for establishing political, diplomatic and commercial relations between the two countries. In addition, the Saudi and Persian monarchs exchanged congratulatory telegrams acknowledging the beginning of official diplomatic relations. In March 1930 the Shah appointed Habibollah Khan Hoveida as his Minister in Jeddah.[66]

2
A Comparison of the Political Systems

The processes of nation-building in what would become Saudi Arabia and Iran, described briefly in the previous chapter, were significant not only in themselves, but also in the fact that they occurred at a time when nearly all Middle Eastern countries were still under colonial rule. By 1932 both countries under their respective monarchs were internationally recognized as fully sovereign and independent states.[1] Before turning to the next stage of their relations, however, it would be helpful to review the political systems that developed in the two countries. This chapter will examine and compare the nature of the political systems and structures in both Saudi Arabia and Iran.

The Saudi Political System

The Saudi political system is in a real sense a reflection of the social structure of the Kingdom. Basically, Saudi society is traditional and tribal, with tribal and extended family ties of great importance at all levels of society. Saudi society, particularly the Najdi heartland, is also very homogeneous by Middle Eastern standards. Probably its most salient characteristic, however, is its conservative Islamic nature. The impact of Islam on the culture and, by extension, on the daily affairs of all Saudi citizens, cannot be overstated. The vast majority of Saudis are Sunni

Muslims, most of them following the Hanbali school of Islamic jurisprudence and the teachings of the Wahhabi revival movement. There is a significant minority of Shi'a Muslims, nearly all of whom are located in the Eastern Province, particularly in the oases of al-Hasa and al-Qatif.

Besides being family-oriented, Saudi society is highly personalized and nearly all social relationships revolve around the extended family. An important feature is the strict separation of men and women outside the home. Men and women have their own traditional spheres of activity, with women dominant in but restricted to the home and men dominant in public affairs, commerce and other activities in the world outside. In recent years, opportunities for women outside the home have increased,[2] but many still find it difficult to give up an important aspect of the traditional mode of life—their power in the home—for limited social mobility outside. This is because most of Saudi social life is centred around the home.

Despite the modernization process over the last 60 years, traditional Saudi social values are likely to remain, on balance, a stabilizing force in the Kingdom. And the modern political system that has developed in this period is particularly sensitive to those values. The system is virtually unique when compared to other political systems in the Arab or Islamic world.

As an Islamic country ruled by a monarchical system, Saudi Arabia does not have a written constitution. The 'constitution' of the country is the holy Quran—God's final revelation to all people, embodying His divine laws regulating all human activity, whether political, economic or social. As Muslims, Saudis believe that the Quran and the *Sunna* (the inspired teachings of the Prophet Muhammad) provide the basic constitutional framework for establishing the relationship between the governors and the governed. Further, they contain all the necessary guidelines for regulating the daily dealings between the members of its society and define their rights and duties.

Theoretically, the Quran and the *Sunna* provide a total and complete system of laws governing society. In a modern technological world, however, there are an increasing number of activities that require regulation. In the Saudi system, these regulations are issued as *nizams* (royal decrees). They do not have the status of law (i.e. Islamic law), and to be valid, they must conform to Islamic law. A major function of the judiciary is to issue *fatwas* (Islamic legal opinions) on the validity of various decrees or other major government decisions.

The development of a political structure in Saudi Arabia was gradual, largely unplanned and pragmatic. Initially, it was a very personalized rule, by the King and those who had earned his trust, both inside the royal family and outside. The two guiding principles, then and now, were consultation and consensus. Realizing that the Hijaz was more advanced governmentally than Najd, Abd al-Aziz allowed many of its political institutions to remain intact and appointed his son Faisal as Viceroy of the Hijaz in 1925, at the age of 19. With time, Hijazi ministries were submerged into national ministries which were created as the need arose, and by the time of Abd al-Aziz's death in 1953, Saudi Arabia had its first Council of Ministers.

By that time, the basic Saudi political structure was fairly well formed, based on six major institutions:[3] the office of the King; the office of the Crown Prince; the Council of Ministers; the religious establishment; and, closely associated with it, the judicial system; and regional and local government (see Table 2).

The Iranian Political System

Iranian society, like Saudi society, is tribally based, but unlike Saudi society, it is extremely heterogeneous.[4] The bulk of the population belong to a number of separate ethnic groups.[5] The largest group is composed of the Iranians, who are Indo-European (Aryan) and speak various Iranian dialects. They make up over 70 per cent of the population. Iranians are further subdivided into Persians (19 million), Kurds (est. 6 million), Gilanis and Mazandaranis (2.5 million), Lurs (1 million) and Baluchis (500,000).

Ethnic differences among the Iranians are largely linguistic. For example, the Persians speak Persian or Farsi, the principal language of the country. The other Iranian groups speak dialects that are closely related but separate languages. The second largest group are Turkish-speakers, who make up some 26 per cent of the population. They include Azeris (Azerbaijanis) (8.5 million), Qashqa'is (500,000), Turkomans (250,000) and various other tribes (750,000). The remainder of the population are mainly Semitic speakers, including Arabs (1 million), Assyrians and neo-Aramaeans (50,000). There is also a small Jewish community (though many fled the revolution). An Armenian community, numbering about 250,000, is also to be found, mainly in Tehran and in the north-west. There are other differences than linguistic among the population. Most of the Sunnis (approximately 10 per cent of the whole) are found along the Iranian frontiers among the Kurds, the Arabs of Khuzistan and further south along the Gulf coast, and the Baluchis, on the border of Pakistan.

This ethnic heterogeneity presented Riza Shah with far more problems in seeking to unify Persia and maintain internal stability than was the case in Saudi Arabia. Whereas the ethnic homogeneity of Saudi society contributed significantly to the country's social, political, economic and cultural develop-

Table 2. The Six Major Institutions of the Saudi Political Structure

Institution	Specific functions
Office of the King	Executive power; protection of the Islamic community; presides over meetings of the Council of Ministers; foreign ambassadors are accredited to him.
Office of the Crown Prince	The second man in the country; the legal successor to the King; presides over meetings of the Council of Ministers when the King is absent.
The Council of Ministers	Considered as the legislative branch; sets internal and external policies; meets on a weekly basis; approves treaties and international agreements; possesses regulatory, executive and administrative authority.
The religious	Divided into three levels: (a) the Imam, institutions; (b) the *alim*; and (c) the *mutawa'*, to guard the purity of the faith and enforce the observation of Islamic law. Have influence over: (a) the judicial system; (b) religious education; (c) the supervision of girls' education; and (d) the handling of legal cases in courts and many other religious aspects.
The judiciary and law courts	Implements *Shari'a* as the basic law of the Kingdom; has a well-developed system of legal courts, presided over by highly experienced and educated *qadis*, who see that justice is observed.
The regional governments	Administered by *amirs*; constitute the link between the regions and central government; responsible to the Minister of Interior; empowered to furnish financial assistance to social and charitable organizations; have provincial council to serve the interests of the population.

A Comparison of the Political Systems

ment, the ethnic heterogeneity in Persia was a major destabilizing factor. For example, before consolidating his power, Riza Pahlavi had first to subdue local anti-government rebellions in Khorrasan (a region adjacent to the Soviet border of Turkistan),[6] Azerbaijan, Kurdistan and Turkistan.[7]

Despite the centrifugal forces of a heterogeneous society, Riza Pahlavi succeeded in establishing a strong central government. Again, the task before him was different from that of Abd al-Aziz in that Riza Khan inherited a political structure that was already fairly sophisticated whereas Abd al-Aziz did not. By 1928 Riza Shah had built on this structure a constitutional monarchy with a cabinet form of government, a two-house legislature (a lower house called the Majlis and an upper house called the Senate) and an independent judiciary. Despite the trappings of democracy, however, he maintained virtual absolute control of the government by manipulation of a one-party system.[8] He filled the parliament with loyal followers and kept for himself key government positions such as Premier, Commander-in-Chief and Minister of War.[9]

Given this background, a number of interesting similarities and differences in how the Iranian and Saudi political systems developed can be identified.

Monarchical Systems

Although Abd al-Aziz and Riza Shah both developed monarchical systems, they were far from identical. The Saudi monarchy, in essence, was and remains a consensual system. This means that the legitimacy of the ruler is based on the general consensus of the ruled. This consensus is not just some form of popularity contest, but is based on Islamic law.[10] The King is not above the law and can be sued in his own courts. As a devout follower of the Wahhabi revival movement, Abd al-Aziz was insistent that the Saudi political system conform to Islamic law according to the Hanbali school of jurisprudence. Due to the constraints of consensus and Islamic law, the Saudi monarch is far from the absolute ruler he has been portrayed in the West.

The Persian monarchy of Riza Pahlavi sprang from an altogether different tradition. Although he was a secularist, his country's political traditions were indelibly influenced by Twelver Shi'a Islam, the religion of the great majority of the people. Twelvers believe that the Twelfth Imam miraculously disappeared and will one day reappear to right the wrongs of mankind. Theoretically, though 'hidden', he is still the sole legitimate leader of the faithful; anyone else can, at best, only be his agent. As a result, Persian rulers have traditionally had to claim legitimacy not by appealing to Islamic law, but through the establishment of dictatorial rule. Riza Shah was no exception. Though he decreed that Shi'a Islam was the state religion, he ruled despite it, not under it as Abd al-Aziz attempted to do under Sunni Islam. Thus Riza Shah was indeed as close to an absolute monarch as one could be in the twentieth century.

Cabinets and Councils of Ministers

Differences between the two countries' style of cabinet government were even more pronounced in the 1920s and 1930s. There was already a highly developed cabinet when Riza Pahlavi took over the Persian government and, indeed, he first assumed the premiership in 1923 before replacing the last Qajar Shah.[11] As mentioned previously, Saudi ministries evolved slowly over time and did not coalesce into a Council of Ministers until 1953. King Abd al-Aziz's first step toward the establishment of a Council of Ministers was taken in 1930 when he created a Ministry of Foreign Affairs,[12] closely followed by a Ministry of Finance. Because ministries were created as a result of the natural expansion of areas being centrally administered by the Saudi government, and because many of them predated the Council of Ministers, each ministry operated more or less independently of the others in the early days. Only more recently has the Council of Ministers begun to function more as a single body.

Another distinction between the two systems was that the Saudi cabinet was directly responsible to the King whereas the Persian/Iranian cabinet was responsible to parliament. This was largely a meaningless distinction, however, for Riza Shah controlled parliament and through it the cabinet.

Parliament

Parliamentary development in the two countries was vastly different. Riza Shah inherited a parliament while Saudi Arabia has never had a national parliament. In theory, the purpose of the Persian parliament (which consisted of 280 members, 220 from the Majlis and 60 from the Senate) was to make laws. In practice, it was largely a rubber stamp for approving Riza Shah's wishes.

Had Abd al-Aziz created a parliament, it would not have served the same legislative function. In the Saudi system, the only valid laws are derived from the *Shari'a*. A parliament would serve the function of a consultative assembly or council—a body which, after consultation, would reach a consensus on how to address certain problems. Its decisions would take the form of regulations rather than laws.

Abd al-Aziz did establish a Consultative Council (Majlis al-Shura) for the Hijaz after he conquered it in 1926, and it still exists. Along with another body, the Council of Deputies (Majlis al-Wukala), the Consultative Council governed the affairs of the Hijaz.[13] It was composed of eight members, headed by the Viceroy of the Hijaz, all elected by the *ulama* (religious scholars) and all prominent, capable and respected people in the community.[14] The creation of a national consultative body has been under consideration in Saudi Arabia for quite some time, but many problems, not the least of which concern Islamic law, have to be worked out.

Religious Institutions
Strong religious establishments existed in both Persia and Najd when Riza Pahlavi and Abd al-Aziz came to power. In the broadest terms, the differences in how they were incorporated into the political system sprang from the following factors. The Al Sauds were champions of the Wahhabi revival espoused by the Najdi religious establishment whereas Riza Pahlavi saw the Persian religious establishment as rivals for power. Ever since the Wahhabi revival in the mid-seventeenth century, the Al Sauds had been its champions. Abd al-Wahhab's descendants, know as the Al al-Sheikh, are the second most respected family in the Kingdom after the Al Sauds. It is the partnership of the religious and secular leadership under Islamic law that has provided the continuity, the legitimacy and the ideological appeal of the Saudi monarchy for nearly 250 years.

For Riza Shah, on the other hand, the Persian religious establishment were rivals. They recognized no secular authority at all, and had broadly based support from the people, making them a major threat to his fledgling regime. Thus, while he included constitutional provisions for consultation with the religious establishment in the legislative process and for all laws passed by the Majlis to be consonant with Islamic law,[15] in practice, he sought to undermine the authority of the religious establishment through a combination of trying to co-opt their leaders, creating the image of them as backward and reactionary, or simply ignoring them.

The Judiciary Systems
The differences between the Najdi and Persian judicial systems reflected the differences between their rulers' attitudes towards Islam and the religious establishment. Islam is above all a legal system—a system of God's law. Traditionally, there had developed a system of Islamic justice to administer the law. The court system, known as *qada'* courts, is presided over by a *qadi* (Islamic judge). Islam also provides for *fatwas* given by a *mufti* (legal expert) to be delivered on the legality of acts either taken or contemplated. The Saudi government still requests a *fatwa* for all important decisions. The head of the system was traditionally called the Chief Qadi and Grand Mufti.

Abd al-Aziz inherited an Islamic legal system and left it intact, but there was no organized judiciary. In the absence of judicial courts, the *amirs* (secular administrators) and *qadis* of the cities would investigate the people's claims and disputes. In the villages and small towns, a combination of traditional and Islamic laws was practised by a *qadi* known as *al-'arif* (the one who knows).[16] Both systems lacked binding authority and resulted in a number of unresolved cases.

Thus it was the task of King Abd al-Aziz to create a formally organized judicial system which would make binding rules and decisions. In August 1927 he established the system of *qada'* courts headed by a Chief Qadi and Grand Mufti who was a member of the Al al-Sheikh family.[17] Over the years, the system has been streamlined and modernized, though the law of the courts, Islamic law, remains the same. For example, the office of Chief Qadi and Grand Mufti was subsequently changed to that of Minister of Justice by King Faisal when he consolidated the judicial system into a ministry, but the functions remained the same.

Riza Shah took a totally different direction from Abd al-Aziz. Although the Persian constitution stated that the official religion of the country was Islam, and its true sect the Ja'farrya (i.e. the Twelver Shi'a sect),[18] Riza Shah created a secular judicial system based on a modified form of French civil law (Code Napoléon). In doing so, he hoped to challenge the competence of the religious courts in civil matters and indirectly aimed at depriving the Persian Shi'a clergy of their socially recognized influence. As previously mentioned, the Shah saw these clergymen as unprogressive and as representing major obstacles to his efforts to Westernize his country.

Regional Government and Political Parties
Two other contrasting elements of the Persian and Saudi political systems can be mentioned here, regional government and political parties. King Abd al-Aziz developed a far more decentralized political system than Riza Shah. He created regional and municipal administrators to whom he delegated considerable powers, the most important positions generally going to members of the Al Sauds. For example, his son Faisal was appointed Viceroy of the Hijaz, and a cousin, Abdallah ibn Jilawi Al Saud, was appointed Amir of the Eastern Province. Another member of the ibn Jilawi branch of the family was appointed Amir of Ha'il, home of the Al Rashids, former rivals to the Al Sauds. All wielded considerable independent powers. Other posts were given to those outside the royal family who were trusted followers. Abd al-Aziz's decision to delegate so much power to these regional administrators was due to the vastness of his Kingdom and the difficulties in communications: to be able to rule over such a wide range of territory, he needed a regional government system. However, all these administrators ruled in the King's name and followed his instructions.

A Comparison of the Political Systems

In comparison, Riza Shah created a highly centralized system with a minimum of delegation of powers. Well aware that he had many rivals and was not trusted, he did not extend his trust beyond a small circle of loyal followers. Thus he resorted to force and military power in order to rule the country and solve his border problems with neighbouring countries.

A second major difference in the political systems developed by the two leaders concerned the creation of political parties. Riza Shah saw the usefulness of a political party in creating mass support, but did not believe that democratic institutions could work in Persian society.[19] Thus he created a single-party system—Rastakhiz (Resurgence)—and controlled it personally. The existence of only one party, however, prompted the creation of a large number of underground parties, many of which were affiliated to foreign countries and ideologies. The Communist Party of Iran (Hezb-e Komonist-e Iran), established in 1917 by a group of Persians working in the oil industry at Baku (Russia),[20] was forced to go underground. Other political groups, such as the National Liberation Movement, followed suit and activated their underground operations. As a result, the political arena was divided between one official legal party, the Rastakhiz, and a number of illegal underground parties.

With no parliament, there was never any reason to have political parties in Saudi Arabia. Moreover, King Abd al-Aziz felt that the Kingdom's tribal base enabled everyone to have an equal say through tribal channels. In addition, with such a small population, he believed that he could maintain a direct personal relationship between rulers and the ruled. The preference for personalized responses persists within Saudi society to this day.

The dictatorial political system created by Riza Shah remained very shaky and unstable. Intermittently, it had to face new challenges, political as well as religious. After Riza Shah was forced to abdicate in 1941, his son and successor, Muhammad Riza Shah, faced similar challenges. He was forced into exile from 1951 to 1953, and in 1979 the monarchy was finally overthrown. The political system created by his father has to a great degree been supplanted by the constitution of the Islamic Republic.

In Saudi Arabia, there have been great changes in the size and scale of government operations. Development in the political, economic, social, cultural and military domains has obliged the ruling family further to develop and modernize its public administration. For example, the number of ministries has been revised several times, and many new boards and agencies have been created to deal with contemporary problems.

Despite all these changes, however, the basic political system in Saudi Arabia has remained largely unchanged since the reign of King Abd al-Aziz. It is still an Islamic monarchy under the rule of Islamic law and governed through consultation and consensus. And despite all the changes in Iran, from a secular monarchy to an Islamic Republic, the dictatorial nature of the regime, depriving citizens of basic human rights, has changed very little from that of its predecessor. The secret police is as alive and well today as it was in the 1920s. Moreover, the current rulers believe that their political system is the only truly Islamic one and should be exported all over the Muslim world, through violence if necessary.

Perhaps the ultimate comparison of the two political systems, therefore, is not one of institutions or structure, but one of intent. As King Faisal of Saudi Arabia once said:

> The important thing about a regime is not what it is called but how it acts. There are corrupt republican regimes and sound monarchies and vice versa. The only true criterion of a regime—whether it be monarchical or republican—is the degree of reciprocity between ruler and ruled and the extent to which it symbolizes prosperity, progress, and healthy initiative... The quality of a regime should be judged by its deeds and the integrity of its rulers, not by its name.[21]

3
Foreign Policy and Bilateral Foreign Relations 1932–82

Saudi Arabia's relations with Iran in the years 1932–82 can be divided into four major periods corresponding to the reigns of King Abd al-Aziz, King Saud, King Faisal and King Khalid. For Iran, the period covers the reigns of Riza Shah and Muhammad Riza Shah, and the first three years of the republic under Ayatollah Khomeini.

A Period of Ups and Downs (1932–41)

Following the unification process that culminated in the creation of the Kingdom of Saudi Arabia in 1932, King Abd al-Aziz turned his attention to consolidating his gains through internal reforms and improving external relations. Realizing the crucial need to participate in world affairs, he focused his attention first on bilateral relations between his newly created kingdom and neighbouring states, including Iran.[1]

The course of those relations was strongly influenced by the foreign-policy styles and objectives of Abd al-Aziz and Riza Shah. For his part, Abd al-Aziz's foreign policy reflected his personal journey from traditional Arab culture to the stage of world politics, a journey throughout which he struggled to remain loyal to both systems. Jacob Goldberg describes the changes undergone by the self-educated King Abd al-Aziz:

Ibn Saud was a desert ruler, albeit of genius, who had no personal political experience of the world outside the confines of Arabia. Yet for some reason he was able to grasp the complexities of international politics before, on the eve of, and during World War I. He mastered the art of diplomatic negotiations with all the linguistic nuances and subtlety that it entailed.[2]

King Abd al-Aziz quickly learned to approach foreign-policy problems with flexibility and pragmatism. For example, he was acutely aware of British interests and military superiority in the Arabian/Persian Gulf region, so he avoided serious confrontation with Britain despite territorial disputes with Bahrain and the Trucial States involving historic Saudi claims.[3] The King's pragmatism led him to recognize that political means are more effective than force when one's adversary can wield greater force, so in 1927 he signed a non-aggression treaty with the British that covered all Arab Gulf sheikhdoms.

It is also important to note that the King's foreign policy was shaped by and reflected his commitment to Islamic law, a commitment that revealed his sometimes divided loyalties to the traditional and modern worlds. Abd al-Aziz sought to reach out to the outside world without interrupting the traditional and Islamic way of life inside his kingdom. By 1932 his foreign-policy objectives could be summed up as seeking good relations with all the states with which Saudi Arabia came into contact. He hoped to support world peace and to strengthen his ties with Europe and the United States, while at the same time building closer relations with the states in the Islamic world. Although he built ties with the West using the tools of Western diplomacy, he also supported Arab unity and opposed continued colonial rule, particularly in Palestine where the large numbers of Jews who had fled from Nazi Germany in the 1930s became increasingly militant in their demand for a zionist state.[4]

Riza Shah also had to straddle two worlds in his foreign policy, but he chose to do so with a different style. Whereas King Abd al-Aziz sought to create consensus, Riza Shah's foreign policy was marked by an independence that was sometimes seen as hostile isolationism. The Shah was more willing than Abd al-Aziz to engage in confrontation to advance his interests, as when he challenged Britain by claiming that Bahrain and other Gulf islands belonged to Iran. He participated in Islamic world politics on a lower level than King Abd al-Aziz, no doubt partly because of Iran's unique status in the region as a non-Arab, Muslim nation. Riza Shah was also inclined to seek his own way in his European alliances, as shown by his relations with Nazi Germany.[5] His policies had the long-term consequence of estranging him both from the Arabs, who resented his lack of involvement in the struggle for independence from the colonial powers, and from the European Allied powers, who remembered his ties to Germany.

There were nevertheless formal Saudi–Persian ties during the period. King Abd al-Aziz's wish to avoid antagonizing Riza Shah as he carried out his preferred course of negotiating with the British led him to sign the Treaty of Friendship in 1929.[6] The treaty led to improved relations and in March 1930 a Persian Embassy was established in Jeddah. A British diplomatic report from Jeddah indicates that the Saudi delegation sent to Tehran to negotiate the Friendship Treaty originally proposed an alliance under which each country would materially assist the other in case of attack. The proposal was apparently rejected by the Persian government[7] and the two countries agreed to the less binding promise of non-aggression. If true, the report of the proposed mutual-defence treaty would show another facet of Abd al-Aziz's delicately balanced foreign policy.

In an effort further to solidify Saudi–Persian relations, King Abd al-Aziz sent his son Prince Faisal ibn Abd al-Aziz (later King Faisal), Viceroy of the Hijaz, on a six-day goodwill mission to Tehran in May 1932, the first high-ranking visit between the two countries.[8] During the visit, Prince Faisal met with Riza Shah and delivered a personal message from the King. He also discussed bilateral political relations and the Persian annual pilgrimage to Makkah and Madinah with the Shah and Persian Foreign Ministry officials, talks that were described in diplomatic parlance as successful and fruitful. Although Riza Shah did not return the visit,[9] Saudi–Iranian relations were active in the years leading up to the Second World War. The two countries made constant contacts relating to regional and bilateral issues. Also, both countries followed the rapidly deteriorating political and military situation in Europe.

In 1939 both Saudi Arabia and Iran announced their neutrality towards the war and the warring nations. However, the European Allies, including the Soviet Union, whose suspicions were aroused by Iran's pre-war relations with Germany,[10] perceived that Iran's neutrality might conflict with their interests and military strategy. This perception led to the Allies' occupation of Iran in 1941, which forced Riza Shah to abdicate in favour of his 23-year-old son, Muhammad Riza.

For King Abd al-Aziz the situation was different. He maintained normal, although far from warm, diplomatic and commercial relations with Germany until 1941, when he ended the Kingdom's neutrality and sided with the European Allies. In so doing, he gained the confidence of the Allied powers—particularly Britain and later the United States—and precluded the possibility of an Allied occupation of Saudi Arabia. The Allies benefited from the Kingdom's alliance by gaining access to the country's oil supplies and to its seaports on the Red Sea and the Arabian/Persian Gulf.

New Directions, New Problems (1941-53)

In both political and military terms, the Second World War was a crucial test for the Saudi and Iranian regimes. The Saudi monarchy came out of the war stronger and more politically confident, and it enjoyed a high degree of political stability in the post-war era. The Iranian monarchy had a more difficult time. The Allied occupation, by the Russians in the north and the British in the south, undermined the political identity of the inexperienced new Shah, Muhammad Riza Shah Pahlavi, who was in the unenviable position of reigning without ruling. Iran emerged from the war with a damaged economy, a fragmented military force and the potential for domestic political instability.

Saudi-Iranian political relations remained cool but stable until December 1943, when the Saudi police arrested an Iranian *hajji* (pilgrim) inside the Great Mosque in Makkah for throwing excrement at the Ka'bah.[11] He was tried, found guilty and executed in accordance with the *Shari'a*.[12] Reaction to this incident quickly threatened the Friendship Treaty that had kept the two countries at arm's length since 1929. The Iranian Embassy in Saudi Arabia vigorously protested at the beheading of the pilgrim in a letter to the Saudi Arabian Foreign Ministry dated 12 December 1943.[13] The letter denounced the execution as illegal and against human law and threatened repercussions by saying that 'the Embassy reserves the entire rights of the Iranian State regarding this regrettable occurrence and all consequences which may ensue'.

Angered by the inflammatory tone of the Iranian letter, the Saudi Foreign Ministry responded in kind:

> The Iranian Legation has arranged the shape of the crime committed by one of the Iranian pilgrims as it likes and has considered it as being contrary to religious and Islamic law. If the Iranian Legation had inquired about the matter and knew the truth of it, it would not have been so hasty in sending this note.[14]

Iran's answer came a month later, on 2 February 1944. The Iranian Embassy in Saudi Arabia reiterated its condemnation of the Saudi government's action in a three-page letter that ended with a threat to sever diplomatic ties:

Foreign Policy and Bilateral Foreign Relations 1932–82

As long as Iranian spirits and honour are not protected in the lands of the Kingdom of Saudi Arabia, and if necessary reparations are not made to the Iranian Government regarding this unheard-of event for which no name can be found in international relations, the Iranian Government considers itself obliged to review the continuance of its relation with the Government of Saudi Arabia.[15]

This led to the two nations' recalling their representatives and breaking off diplomatic relations in March 1944. A minor dispute then arose over who should represent Iranian interests in Saudi Arabia. Iran suggested that it would entrust them to Egypt's legation in the Kingdom, a proposal accepted by King Abd al-Aziz. Soon afterwards, however, the Iranian representative in Baghdad asked that the Iraqi legation be allowed to represent his country's interests. This request was rejected by King Abd al-Aziz because of the unsettled border disputes between Saudi Arabia and Iraq.[16] Iran eventually entrusted its interests in the Kingdom to the Egyptian Embassy, while Lebanon represented Saudi interests in Tehran.

The estrangement continued until 15 October 1946, when King Abd al-Aziz wrote a personal letter to Shah Muhammad Riza Pahlavi, urging the renewal of Saudi–Iranian relations and asking that they be based on old and faithful ties.[17] The fact that the King took the initiative in renewing diplomatic relations, even though Iran had severed them, indicates his willingness to put regional peace and Arab unity ahead of lesser interests. The Shah responded favourably to King Abd al-Aziz's letter and expressed his desire to resolve the misunderstanding. Saudi–Iranian diplomatic relations were resumed in early 1947.[18]

Between 1947 and 1950 Saudi–Iranian relations strengthened as the interests of the countries merged in two important areas. First, Iran decisively aligned itself with Western, particularly American, interests. Second, as the two countries developed their oil industries, they often dealt with common issues. The parallel development of the two nations was disrupted in 1951, however, by the turbulent state of Iran's internal politics. In March of that year the Shah had to flee Iran, not to return until August 1953 when assistance from the United States enabled him to regain power. Even during his absence, however, diplomatic relations between Iran and Saudi Arabia continued: in the autumn of 1951 Iran assigned Mozaffar Alam as Ambassador Extraordinary and Plenipotentiary to Saudi Arabia.[19]

The year 1953 saw the death of King Abd al-Aziz ibn Abd al-Rahman Al Saud, founder and father of the Kingdom of Saudi Arabia. His passing ushered in a new era in Saudi–Iranian political relations.

Saudi–Iranian Relations 1932–1982

The Era of Give and Take (1953–64)

With the return of Muhammad Riza Pahlavi as Shah of Iran in 1953 and the succession of King Saud ibn Abd al-Aziz to the Saudi throne as the eldest son of the founder of modern Saudi Arabia, Saudi–Iranian political relations began to evolve around three major issues: regional politics, oil[20] and international security.

King Saud, like his father King Abd al-Aziz, recognized the importance of maintaining good relations with Iran, sometimes even at the risk of jeopardizing other Saudi interests. For example, both King Abd al-Aziz and King Saud viewed the pro-communist attempts to overthrow the Shah in 1951 and 1953 as a serious threat to regional security. The Kingdom nevertheless refrained from interfering in Iran's internal affairs, choosing instead to follow a policy of 'wait and see'.

The Saudi policy of non-interference was not an obstacle to resuming normal relations upon Shah Muhammad Riza's return from exile because the Shah was also eager to pursue strong bilateral ties. He saw that his prestige at home and within the region depended partly on the strength of his relations with the Kingdom of Saudi Arabia. Moreover, it quickly became apparent that Saudi Arabia and Iran, bound as they were by their common economic stakes in the oil industry, would have common interests in many of the region's political developments, such as the British role in the Arabian/Persian Gulf, the Nasserist movement in Egypt,[21] the situation in Turkey and the political situation in the states of the Fertile Crescent.

In the international arena, both countries strengthened their relations with the Western world in the period following the Second World War. With the establishment of the United Nations in 1945, both Saudi Arabia and Iran became active members, abiding by its Charter and related international treaties and agreements.[22]

These constructive steps in Saudi–Iranian relations led the Shah to invite King Saud to pay a state visit to Iran in August 1955. The visit was the first of its kind between the two countries since their creation as fully independent, sovereign states. During the visit, which lasted almost a week, the two monarchs discussed a variety of political, economic, security and military issues. They agreed on the dangers of communism and the particular threats it posed to Middle Eastern nations, and expressed a common willingness to join the West in combating it. They were also in agreement that the Islamic countries needed to solve their regional disputes. Last but not least, they discussed the Baghdad Pact.[23]

The discussion of the Baghdad Pact caused some disagreement. This arose from King Saud's belief at the time (immediately after the pact was signed) that it included secret clauses in favour of Israel.²⁴ The King elaborated on his position in April 1956 in a conversation with the Iranian Ambassador to Egypt, which took place in Saudi Arabia. He said that while he had nothing against the Baghdad Pact as such, he understood that it included secret clauses that operated to the detriment of the Arab states and in favour of Israel.²⁵ The issue did not deter the two monarchs, however, from publishing a bilateral communiqué reiterating the two nations' friendship and calling for more co-operation in political, economic and security areas.

Despite the note of public optimism that concluded the visit, a number of important political issues, such as Iran's claim to Bahrain, were left unresolved. Moreover, there were reports that the visit had not gone well on the personal level. King Saud was reportedly angry at the unenthusiastic reception he had received in Iran and at the country's adherence to the Baghdad Pact. After the visit the King ordered the Saudi authorities in Dhahran not to admit Bahrainis whom they suspected of being of Persian origin or having Persian names.²⁶ Back in Iran, the Shah granted an American journalist a private interview in which he expressed distaste and surprise at seeing King Saud's private secretary kneeling on the floor of the car beside the King. The Shah added that he would never demand that kind of subservience.²⁷ Despite the petty antagonism that grew out of King Saud's visit, Saudi–Iranian relations continued undisturbed as both countries realized the necessity for co-operation in matters of mutual concern.

One notable area of co-operation was the United Nations. In January 1956 Saudi Arabia sought and obtained Iranian support when it brought the issue of its claim to the Buraimi oasis to the attention of the UN Security Council. The oasis is situated between Saudi Arabia, the Sultanate of Oman and the Emirate of Abu Dhabi (now part of the United Arab Emirates).²⁸ Iran, at the same time, needed Saudi support in its grievances over Britain's treatment of Iranians in Bahrain and other parts of the Gulf region.²⁹

Despite this co-operation, the differences between Iran and Saudi Arabia were never far from the surface, as was shown by the Suez crisis of 1956. Some observers believe that the Shah's feelings towards the Arabs were influenced by his marriage to Princess Fawziah, the sister of King Farouq of Egypt. Princess Fawziah was not happy with her marriage, and frequently expressed her unhappiness by means of unflattering comparisons of Tehran with cosmopolitan Cairo.³⁰ Resentment at her outspokenness may have contributed to the Shah's decision to remain on the sidelines when the Arab world and many Islamic countries condemned the invasion of Egypt.³¹ In any event, the Suez crisis strained relations between Arab and non-Arab Muslims.

The strain was eased somewhat by Shah Muhammad Riza Pahlavi's visit to Saudi Arabia in 1957. King Saud first extended an oral invitation via the Iranian Ambassador to Egypt during their meeting in Jeddah on 24 April 1956.[32] On 25 October he followed this up with a formal written invitation. During the six-day visit, which began on 12 March 1957, the Shah was accompanied by thirty officials, including the Foreign Minister, the Minister of Court and the President of the Iranian Senate.[33] The Shah and his delegation flew directly to Riyadh, where they spent three days and nights. From Riyadh, they flew to Jeddah, from where they travelled by car to Makkah and Madinah, returning to the Saudi capital on 17 March, one night before their departure for Iran.[34]

During the official talks, the Baghdad Pact was again an issue. King Saud protested that one of its signatories, Britain, had attacked an Arab country, Egypt, but he did not criticize the overall pact. On the contrary, he raised the possibility of improved relations with Iraq, which was a member of the pact. The heads of state also discussed the Shah's suggestion of a Saudi–Iranian Defence Pact, aimed particularly at detaching Saudi Arabia from Egypt and Syria and at improving the standing of the Baghdad Pact in the Arab world.[35] King Saud did not reject the idea and promised to study it.

King Saud and the Shah also discussed Saudi–British relations, which had been damaged both by the dispute over the Buraimi oasis and by the Suez crisis. King Saud said that he understood British interests in the Middle East and hinted that he would consider resuming relations with Britain if it approached him with a concrete proposal regarding the Buraimi oasis. The Shah suggested that Saudi Arabia and Britain might negotiate the matter through a third country such as Switzerland.[36]

Other issues, such as the future of a number of islands in the Gulf, peace and security in the Middle East, the Palestinian question and co-operation among the Muslim nations, were also on the agenda. The two leaders released a joint communiqué at the conclusion of the visit.[37] At the time, it was reported to have been an unparalleled success.

Saudi–Iranian political relations in the aftermath of the Shah's visit to Saudi Arabia did indeed witness a remarkable improvement. Political co-operation and identical political views began to evolve around the critical issues of the era. As an example, both countries had similar views on the Lebanese crisis of 1958, and both monarchs embraced the idea of a strong Western move in support of President Cham'oun, who was considered a friend of the West. Moreover, they resisted Soviet attempts to infiltrate the Middle East and united their efforts to stand against President Gamal Abd al-Nasser's revolutionary slogans in the region. Further, King Saud and the Shah shared the view that Nasser was responsible for bringing the Soviet

Union into the region.[38] The two countries adopted a low-key policy *vis-à-vis* the Arabian/Persian Gulf sheikhdoms that aimed to offset Egyptian influence in the region.

Moreover, the two monarchs shared a common concern over the situation in Iraq after its monarchical system had been overthrown in 1958 and replaced by a revolutionary republican regime. However much King Saud disliked the coup, he was not entirely disheartened at the change of regime in Iraq. The new regime in Baghdad would be more dedicated to the concerns of the Arab world, less dependent on the British and less closely identified with the Baghdad Pact.[39]

The strength of Saudi-Iranian relations was put to the test in July 1960, when the Shah made a confusing statement that Iran had extended *de facto* recognition to Israel in 1950.[40] The news media, United Press among them, simply reported that Iran had recognized Israel without making clear that the Shah was speaking about 1950 and without transmitting other remarks by the Shah that assured his audience that he was not announcing a change in Iranian-Israeli relations.[41] (In April 1960 the Shah had intended to exchange ambassadors with Israel in response to what he perceived as Egypt's provocative support for Iraq in its border dispute with Iran.[42] He reconsidered after King Hussein's state visit to Tehran.)

The Shah's statement roused the anger of Egyptian President Nasser and other Arab League members who demanded the breaking-off of diplomatic relations between the Arab world and Iran. King Saud was among the Arab leaders not involved in the move to cut off Iran, but the controversy brought another issue to the forefront, Iran's supply of oil to Israel. These two issues were discussed at a meeting of the Arab League Foreign Ministers in Beirut on 22 August 1960. During this meeting, the Foreign Ministers of the United Arab Republic (UAR[43]) told the other Arab ministers that the UAR expected them to break off diplomatic relations with Iran, and that the UAR would not change its policy towards Iran regardless of what other Arab states decided.[44]

Iran immediately ordered its ambassadors to various Arab countries, including Saudi Arabia, to explain that there was nothing new in the *de facto* recognition. The Shah also exchanged letters with King Hussein of Jordan as part of his effort to mend fences:

There has been no change in Iran's relations with Israel, which have been from the beginning a *de facto* recognition... Such recognition, whether legal or official, has never been a subject of discussion. We must, however, point out that the Iranian government has always shown its good intentions towards the Arab states with which it is linked by religion...[45]

Iran also clarified its position directly to the Arab League by promising not to recognize Israel *de jure* or to exchange envoys. These Iranian efforts made it possible for the Lebanese Foreign Minister who presided over the Arab League Foreign Ministers' meeting to present a conciliatory formula which was accepted by the delegates. The ministers thanked the UAR for its stand in defence of the Arab cause and also thanked Iran for clarifying its position.

For Saudi Arabia, the issue was delicate because of its desire to maintain good relations with Iran without compromising its position in the Arab world. An Iranian decision to extend *de jure* recognition of Israel and the exchange of ambassadors would have forced the Kingdom to choose one side or the other.

Once the episode was over, the Kingdom resumed normal contacts with Iran and in 1962 Iran appointed its eighth ambassador, Afrassial Navai, to Saudi Arabia.[46] The ambassadorial change was recognition that Iran had increasingly come to view Saudi Arabia as an oasis of stability in the region. When asked on 11 April 1962 about his country's relations with the Arab world, Iran's Prime Minister Ali Amini said:

> The Arab countries seem to be getting more and more unstable with the exception of Saudi Arabia which I have heard is in good shape. Nasser is fomenting all this disorder now that he has virtually ruined his own country. I hear that conditions in Egypt are very bad. Iran must save itself from being infected by the disorders in the rest of the Middle East.[47]

Subsequent events in North Yemen further cemented Saudi–Iranian relations. On 19 September 1962 a military *coup d'état* in North Yemen overthrew the Imamate and replaced it with a republican system hostile to Saudi Arabia. When they discovered that the coup had been instigated by President Nasser, Saudi Arabia and Iran withheld recognition from the new regime. Later, when Nasser intervened militarily in North Yemen, Saudi Arabia and Iran extended political and military assistance to the ex-Imam of Yemen, who was fighting to regain his throne.[48] Further evidence that Nasser's adventurism served to cement Saudi–Iranian relations may be discerned in Shah Muhammad Riza's 20 November 1962 interview with the chief editor of *Foreign Reports Bulletin* in which he expressed his worries over the Egyptian intervention in Yemen. According to the Shah, the intervention was aimed at Saudi Arabia and at gaining control of the Arabian peninsula's oil reserves.[49]

Prince Faisal's rise to the Saudi throne in 1964 set the stage for a new era in Saudi-Iranian political relations. Faisal quickly emerged, even before becoming King, as the leader who would counter President Nasser's ambitions.

The Era of Competition and Friendship (1964-75)

With the accession of King Faisal ibn Abd al-Aziz to the Saudi throne on 29 October 1964, Saudi-Iranian political relations began to take on a new look. King Faisal was well known to the Shah of Iran and to many of his government officials, who also held a high opinion of the King's competence as a statesman. In March 1964 the Shah had sent his Foreign Minister to Saudi Arabia to confer with the then Prince Faisal. Upon his return to Tehran, the Iranian Foreign Minister stated that he was immensely impressed by the Prince.[50]

There was friction nevertheless. On the one hand, the leaders in Riyadh and Tehran felt the need to establish closer ties in order to co-ordinate their oil policies within the Organization of Petroleum Exporting Countries (OPEC), to stop President Nasser's moves into the Arabian/Persian Gulf region, and to maintain peace and security in the Middle East in general. On the other hand, full co-operation was not possible because of the two leaders' world views. The Shah of Iran reasoned in geopolitical terms, which included a relationship with Israel; King Faisal thought in pan-Islamic terms,[51] which made Iran's relationship with Israel a real obstacle. He wanted to avoid any setback or deterioration in Saudi Arabia's relations with other Arab states. Fortunately, each monarch recognized the other's situation. The Shah and his Foreign Minister realized that King Faisal could not move closer to Iran without jeopardizing his position in the Arab world. This understanding led Saudi Arabia and Iran to conduct their bilateral relations cautiously and quietly. For a time, both were careful to side-step issues that could embarrass the other.

In 1965, however, the Shah's vision of Iran's future global importance placed an additional strain on Saudi-Iranian relations. Iran, he incorrectly predicted, would develop as the most stable and important country in the region until its prominence on the west side of Asia matched Japan's importance on the east.[52] Furthermore the Shah had a mystic faith that he was guarded by higher powers, a belief strengthened by his surviving an assassination attempt in April 1965.[53] Many Arab leaders resented the Shah's increasing self-importance.

Despite the Shah's posturing attitude, he viewed King Faisal as the only Arab leader able to stand against Nasser, so he continued to co-operate with him. He was willing to extend any help Saudi Arabia required, including the active participation of the Iranian armed forces,[54] in fighting Nasser in Yemen or elsewhere. Although King Faisal was grateful for the Shah's assurances of support, he made it clear that the Shah should avoid the appearance of intervening in any Arab country. He also urged the Iranian parliament to appease the Arab world by renouncing its claim over Bahrain and abolishing the vacant seats it held for representatives from the 'lost province' of Bahrain.[55]

Aside from the Arabian/Persian Gulf region issues and Middle East questions, the two countries expressed common support for Pakistan both during and after its 1965 war with India over the province of Kashmir. Both felt that Pakistan had been betrayed by the Western powers. They also felt that it was important to support Pakistan as an active member of the Central Treaty Organization (CENTO) pact and, more importantly, a Muslim state.

Iran and Saudi Arabia were further united by King Faisal's efforts to visit Islamic countries not only as an Arab King, but as the Custodian of the Holy Cities of Makkah and Madinah. He saw his visits as a way to remind Islamic countries that their primary identity was as Muslims. The King formally initiated his Islamic solidarity policy in 1964, and he conducted his successful tour of the Islamic world in 1965–67. Naturally, Iran was one of his first stops.

King Faisal's visit to Iran in December 1965 followed Iranian Foreign Minister Abbas Aram's visit to the Kingdom in April 1964.[56] The Shah and his ministers were eager to co-operate with the King's vision of an Islamic grouping. In addition, they affirmed their agreement on practical concerns in the Gulf region such as the situation in North Yemen, President Nasser's moves in the Middle East, the oil issue and the Soviets' ambitions in the region. The two monarchs also reached an agreement over the continental shelf and worked out a demarcation pact, which was not signed.[57] Finally, they agreed to establish an Iran–Arab Friendship Association, chaired by Prime Minister Hoveida and with two main branches, one in Tehran and the other in Riyadh.[58]

On his return to Saudi Arabia, King Faisal expressed his satisfaction with the Shah's understanding of the situation in the Arabian peninsula, the Middle East and the Islamic world. He had been able to strengthen his bond with the Iranians without antagonizing the Arabs. Following his successful visit to Iran, King Faisal paid similar visits to Jordan, Sudan and Pakistan.

Iran welcomed those visits and described them as 'a step to prepare the ground for the unity of Islamic countries'.[59] The Shah nevertheless expressed concern that activities on behalf of Islam could be represented as reactionary. In a private talk, he said that 'he was afraid that a false impression would be created that Islam is opposed to real progress and that the Islamic grouping is a club of Kings, and he hoped that King Faisal would stress a modern Islam and show how it could be used to further true progress'.[60]

After the King's visit, Iran was more willing to support Saudi Arabia in public. In June 1966 the Iranian press criticized the mayor of New York City for his rudeness towards King Faisal during the King's visit to the United States.[61] This Iranian position encouraged the acting Saudi Foreign Minister to pay an official five-day visit to Tehran. At the formal airport reception on 21 June 1966, Sayyed Omar al-Saggaf said that the Iranian–Saudi friendship was a perfect example of Islamic brotherhood and neighbourly relations.[62]

The acting Saudi Foreign Minister's visit to Tehran came at a crucial time because it coincided with the deterioration of Iran's political relations with Iraq. In a meaningful juxtaposition, the Shah compared Iran's border dispute with Iraq to Saudi Arabia's dispute with Yemen. He saw Iraq as his Yemen. One purpose of al-Saggaf's visit was to cool down the Iraqi–Iranian border tension. As far back as January 1966 King Faisal had considered hosting a tripartite meeting between the leaders of Iran, Iraq and Kuwait to settle their border disputes and relieve Iranian–Arab tension.[63] The meeting never materialized and shuttle diplomacy was practised instead.

Despite the co-operation, King Faisal and Shah Muhammad Riza Pahlavi never did agree on their approaches to some problems. Iran under the Shah never joined the non-aligned movement, for example, whereas Saudi Arabia was and still is a full member.[64] They also differed on the appropriateness of force in settling regional disputes, with the Shah being less hesitant to use force, as evidenced by his reaction to Britain's announcement of its intention to withdraw from the Arabian/Persian Gulf by the end of 1971. The Shah prepared his armed forces to act as 'policeman' of the Gulf. In addition, he ordered his police intelligence security organization, SAVAK, to conduct operations in the Gulf sheikhdoms.

King Faisal nevertheless succeeded in defusing some of the Shah's aggressive behaviour towards Iraq. He was also able to secure the Shah's support for the ex-Imam of North Yemen, who was fighting to regain his lost throne in the aftermath of the 1962 Egyptian-inspired coup. The King had also succeeded in securing the Shah's support for his call for Islamic solidarity and for support for the Palestinian cause.

The different approaches did not affect the two countries' common goals. The British withdrawal from South Arabia, Aden and South Yemen raised shared concerns about a possible Soviet or Nasserist takeover of that vital part of the Arabian peninsula. The two countries also expressed anxiety over the trouble in Jordan during mid-1966, with the Shah stating privately that he was concerned at the possible repercussions in Saudi Arabia.[65]

The Saudi policy of encouraging Iran paid off in the aftermath of the 1967 six-day Arab–Israeli war, when the Shah openly condemned Israel's occupation of Arab land and demanded that Israel immediately vacate the occupied Arab territories.[66] This political position was considered a major change in Iran's foreign policy towards the Arab world, especially in view of its relationship with Israel.

King Faisal rewarded the Iranian response with a visit to Iran in December 1967. The significance of the visit lies in the fact that Iran was sufficiently rehabilitated in the eyes of the Arabs for the King to visit Iran for the express purpose of advancing bilateral interests. (Two years earlier, the bilateral relationship had taken a back seat to the unity of Muslim countries.) In King Faisal's speech to the Iranian parliament, he emphasized Islam as the binding element between the two nations, but he particularly directed his speech to the Shah, who was present at the Parliament Hall, saying, 'Now is the time for more co-operation and co-ordination between the two countries.' The visit, which lasted only a few days, served its purpose. The monarchs agreed that their Foreign Ministers would meet occasionally to exchange views. King Faisal also invited the Shah to visit Saudi Arabia the following year.

Despite the constructive course of Saudi–Iranian political relations after King Faisal's rise to power in 1964, a degree of restraint could be sensed between the two countries. Certainly, the two monarchs' desire for mutual co-operation was there; but national pride and national interests were much more important than their personal desire for full co-operation. Those different interests led to an unpleasant controversy between the two countries in 1968. In January Saudi Arabia decided to co-ordinate its efforts with Kuwait and Bahrain in order to tackle the expected uncertainties in the Gulf after the British withdrawal in 1971. Iran interpreted such an act as hostile to its own interests in the region and accused both Saudi Arabia and Kuwait of being active in the Gulf in association with Bahrain. This accusation, which the Saudis regarded as unwarranted, caused a setback in Iran's political relations with Saudi Arabia and Kuwait.[67] The Shah kept the matter alive by instructing his ambassadors to Saudi Arabia to complain at the Saudi press's use of the term 'Arabian Gulf' in their daily coverage of the region.[68]

The Shah's efforts to seek Western recognition of Iran's regional influence exacerbated the situation. The Shah wanted the United States to declare that Iran was the only regional power capable of defending the Arab

Gulf sheikhdoms and filling the gap that would be created by the British withdrawal in 1971. (He gained tacit recognition of this status upon the announcement of President Nixon's doctrine of 1969, which called for a reduction in the US military presence abroad by aiding smaller nations to defend themselves through military and economic aid. The Nixon Doctrine enabled the Shah to build up Iran's military capabilities and to act as the legitimate defender of the Gulf region.[69])

The second problem in 1968 arose over the Shah's intended visit to Saudi Arabia. The visit, which had been agreed to during King Faisal's 1967 visit to Tehran, was in due course set for 3–8 February.[70] Suddenly, two days beforehand, while Saudi Arabia was making the final arrangements, the Shah announced that he was cancelling his visit to express Iran's dissatisfaction with Saudi Arabia's activities in the Gulf, including King Faisal's enthusiastic reception of the Amir of Bahrain in January.[71] The Shah's unexpected conduct revived the fading mistrust between Iran and the Arab nations.[72]

Some of the damage was patched up. The Shah realized that he had overreacted and the King was ready to interpret the Shah's action as 'youthful aggressiveness'.[73] The Shah sent a personal messenger to the King in May to request a meeting between the two leaders at Jeddah airport during the Shah's stopover on his way to Ethiopia. King Faisal agreed to meet with the Shah for 40 minutes: when the meeting took place on 3 June, however, it lasted for 5 hours.[74] And at the end of their talks, the two leaders agreed upon a new date, in November, for the Shah to make a formal visit.

The visit took place on schedule. Lasting from 9 to 14 November, the meeting between the two monarchs included the usual issues, but gave special emphasis to international problems like the Palestine question, with both the King and the Shah expressing full support for the Palestinian people, their rights and their claims.[75] The atmosphere was more friendly than might have been expected. During the official dinner at the Malzar Palace, very cordial speeches were exchanged, with the Shah calling King Faisal 'Amir al-Muminin' (the Prince of Believers).[76]

This mutual satisfaction carried over into 1969. The Foreign Ministers of the two countries began to meet periodically and a number of Saudi officials, including members of the royal family, visited Iran. In return, several Iranian officials, such as Dr Manuchehr Igbal, president of the board of directors of the National Iranian Oil Company (NIOC), and the Iranian Minister of Information, visited Saudi Arabia.[77]

The most significant development in 1969 was the meeting between King Faisal and the Shah in the Moroccan capital, Rabat. The occasion was the first Islamic Summit and the celebration of the establishment of the

Organization of the Islamic Conference (OIC). The Shah and the King entered hand in hand and received a standing ovation from an audience that included kings and presidents of the Islamic world.[78]

These positive initiatives and the ability to overcome setbacks set the stage for continued constructive political relations between Saudi Arabia and Iran during the 1970s.

The Decade of Mutual Understanding (the 1970s)

Saudi-Iranian political relations during the first half of the 1970s witnessed a remarkable growth as the countries increasingly learned to co-operate in certain specified areas without letting their disagreements and rivalry disrupt the wider relationship. Several issues emerged as points of contention, however, including the Gulf islands, oil and the communist threat.

The Gulf Islands
Both countries were eager to see a secure and stable Gulf region, particularly after the British withdrawal in 1971. Iran viewed the withdrawal as a problem in the sense that it would require the detection and elimination of coup attempts by extremists with Egyptian and Iraqi support.[79] Saudi Arabia, on the other hand, was concerned at Iranian ambitions to dominate the Gulf militarily and wanted Iranian help in effecting a smooth transfer of power from the British to the traditional rulers of the sheikhdoms. Saudi Arabia therefore opposed Iran's efforts to acquire the islands of Abu Musa and the two Tunbs. In an attempt to resolve this difference, Iranian Foreign Minister Ardashir Zahedi met with King Faisal in Geneva on 17 October 1970, but no final agreement was reached.[80]

The longstanding dispute over Bahrain necessarily became part of the issue. Saudi Arabia was eager to see Bahrain an independent, fully sovereign country, while Iran claimed ownership of the island. From April 1968 the Shah and his officials indicated that their interest in Bahrain was not overriding and that a settlement was possible. One Iranian official went so far as to say:

> [T]he abandonment by Iran of its claim over Bahrain would mean giving up something for nothing. We do not want Bahrain, but our claim to it is an important bargaining point for us in working out the future of the Gulf region.[81]

Such Iranian thinking and statements were considered very healthy by Saudi Arabia, which then designed its Gulf policies accordingly. It was obvious by late 1970 that the Shah was willing to relinquish his claims on Bahrain, but that he would insist on compensation in the form of three other islands, Abu Musa and the two Tunbs. On two occasions, the Shah stated openly that he intended to occupy the three islands by force once the British had withdrawn from the Gulf by the end of 1971.[82]

The Shah's declarations alarmed King Faisal, who did not believe that the Shah could honestly consider these islands to be vital to the security of Iran or the Gulf and saw the Shah's move as economic acquisitiveness. To resolve the problem, the King considered convening a conference on Gulf security, which would have included all interested parties. He thought it important that Iran propose the conference, so on 1 December 1971, King Faisal sent a message explaining his idea to the Shah, who replied that he was interested.[83] Unfortunately, the conference never took place because the Shah had carried out his threat to invade the islands on 30 November.[84] He further threatened to occupy any sheikhdom that fell into the hands of leftist groups or subversive elements. His aggressive policy made it very difficult for Saudi Arabia to co-operate with Iran in the Gulf region.

Iran's invasion of the three islands was, in fact, a face-saving action with economic implications. The Shah wanted to compensate for his loss of Bahrain in the aftermath of the United Nations investigating committee, which had assured itself of the desire of the vast majority of Bahrainis to have their own independent and sovereign state.[85] From the economic viewpoint, the Shah perceived that the islands contained huge reserves of oil and gas. His intentions were clear from the agreement signed with the Amir of Sharjah, the original owner of Abu Musa,[86] which focused more on economic matters than on politics or security.[87] (The Amir of Sharjah was in fact forced to sign the agreement with the Shah despite the fact that he had many historical documents proving the island was an Arab island and belonged to his emirate.)

Oil

The second major point of contention between Iran and Saudi Arabia in the 1970s was oil, particularly the politics of oil. As Saudi Arabia was establishing a linkage between its oil production policy and the Arab–Israeli conflict, the Shah's policies increasingly showed consideration for the American support he received. The situation was complicated even further by Saudi Arabia's desire to meet the oil demands of the West without being unfaithful to the Arab cause, a cause with which King Faisal and his Oil Minister, Sheikh Ahmad Zaki Yamani, repeatedly identified themselves.

Saudi–Iranian Relations 1932–1982

Both Saudi Arabia and Iran are oil-producing countries and depend on oil as their major source of revenue. As early as 1971 the Shah, emboldened by strong US support, began to design an oil policy to challenge that of Saudi Arabia. Saudi Arabia's policy was to link its oil production to the Arab–Israeli conflict. On a number of occcasions, King Faisal and Sheikh Yamani asserted that Saudi Arabia was part of the Arab world and therefore the political climate in the Middle East had to change before Saudi Arabia would increase its oil production to meet the demands of the Western world. Meanwhile the West, especially the United States, was trying to dissociate oil issues from the Arab–Israeli conflict.

The Shah upset this Saudi policy by accepting the American position. He decided not to join Saudi Arabia and the other Arab Gulf oil countries in their oil embargo policy towards supporters of Israel during the 1973 Arab–Israeli war. The Shah viewed oil as merchandise rather than as a political weapon.[88]

The two countries also differed in their pricing policies. Because of the Shah's strictly commercial approach to oil, Iran wanted to raise the price. Saudi Arabia, on the other hand, demanded a decrease. This disagreement was obvious during various OPEC meetings and it grew into a personal clash of interest between the Oil Ministers of Saudi Arabia and Iran. In May 1974, when Sheikh Yamani proposed a reduction in the price of oil by $2.00 a barrel, the Iranian Oil Minister Jamshid Amouzegar opposed the recommendation and accused Yamani of fostering the interests of the oil companies.

Saudi Arabia was none the less keen not to widen the gap with Iran regarding its oil policies and so decided to take Iran into its confidence. In October 1974 Prince Saud al-Faisal, Saudi Deputy Oil Minister, and Omar al-Saggaf, Saudi State Minister for Foreign Affairs, visited Tehran in order to discuss oil prices with the Shah.[89] While he did not entirely agree with the Saudi position of stabilizing and reducing oil prices, the Shah expressed a willingness to review his position. He also promised to co-ordinate his future oil policies with those of the Kingdom. In 1977 the Shah agreed to support the Saudi position by accepting the Saudi–American proposal for freezing oil prices.[90] His decision allowed Iran and Saudi Arabia, the two largest oil producers in OPEC, to co-ordinate their oil policies and seek the stability of the world's economy.

In this matter, the Shah showed his great respect for and admiration of King Faisal throughout the 1960s and the first half of the 1970s, exhibiting a constant willingness to co-operate with the King on regional and Islamic policies. Unfortunately, his co-operation was tempered by considerable personal gamesmanship. It had been noticed that the Shah often made demands and contradicted the Saudi position on particular issues, only to allow himself to be coaxed into moderating his position, without seeming to have any particular policy goals in mind.

The Communist Threat

Both King Faisal and the Shah saw communism as the most dangerous and inhuman form of government, holding it responsible for the spread of leftist and radical regimes in the Arab and the Islamic world. Whereas King Faisal's dislike of communism was based on religious grounds, the Shah's anti-communist stand was based on political reasons. In 1953 the Shah had been in danger of losing his throne because of the alliance between the pro-communist government headed by the Prime Minister Mossadeq and the strong Iranian Communist Party (Tudeh). The Tudeh presented a serious challenge to the Shah and his regime throughout the 1950s and 1960s. It was thus one of the Shah's top priorities in the 1970s to crush the communist movement in Iran and to lessen Soviet influence in his country. To achieve this goal, he relied heavily on his alliance with the United States, which he saw as the ultimate balance against the Soviet Union.

Both King Faisal and the Shah were alarmed by the growth of Soviet power in the Mediterranean and in the Arabian/Persian Gulf region. They were also alarmed by the prospect of the Soviets using American support for Israel to increase their influence on Arab and Muslim nations. In addition, both monarchs were wary of the Soviet and Chinese adventures in Africa. For instance, when the Soviet Union established a sophisticated naval base in Somalia in 1972[91] and used its Cuban proxies to invade Angola in 1977, the two monarchs were greatly disturbed by these two moves and warned the United States of the consequences. These Soviet interventions encouraged Saudi Arabia and Iran to co-ordinate their efforts in fighting communism and its long-term plans for world domination. In 1975 the two countries, joined by Egypt, Morocco and France, decided to establish a secret anti-communist club, formed to combat communism in Asia, Africa and Europe.[92] The club convened its first two-day meeting in Taif, the summer capital of Saudi Arabia. Its subsequent biannual meetings were held in Tehran, Rabat and Nice.

In April 1975 King Faisal of Saudi Arabia was assassinated and a new era of Saudi–Iranian relations began. The Shah paid a two-day visit to the Kingdom on 28–29 April 1975. During this third visit to Saudi Arabia, the Shah extended his condolences to the new Saudi monarch, King Khalid, on the death of King Faisal. He also conducted fruitful discussions with the new Saudi leadership, focusing on bilateral matters, international issues and issues of concern to the whole Islamic world. The two countries also agreed that the security and stability of the Middle East could not be obtained without Israel's withdrawal from all Arab territories, including Jerusalem, occupied during the 1967 Arab–Israeli war, and the restoration of Palestinian rights. At the end of his visit, the Shah extended an invitation to King Khalid to visit Iran.[93]

The Shah's 1975 visit to Saudi Arabia had two important aspects. First, it reflected his respect and admiration for the late King Faisal. Second, it showed his continued interest in a 'special relationship' with the new Saudi leadership. After Nasser's death in 1970, Saudi Arabia and Egypt were the only two Arab countries to have a special relationship with Iran. This does not mean that Iran under the Shah did not have good relations with other Arab countries; on the contrary, the Shah had very close relationships with the Kings of Morocco and Jordan. The difference was that the variety of common interests and their political weight in the Middle East led him to deal differently with Saudi Arabia and Egypt.

From the Saudi point of view, the Shah's 1975 visit was reassurance that he would continue his special relationship with the Kingdom and that he would be willing to enhance their mutual understanding on a number of political, economic and military issues at both the regional and international levels. Among those issues were the security of the Arabian/Persian Gulf, the Arab–Israeli conflict and OPEC policies. Over the next four years, until the fall of the Shah in 1979, the two countries enjoyed a very cordial relationship and were able to achieve sound progress in a number of political, religious and economic areas.

The most important factor behind this progress was the 'oil boom' of the 1970s. In 1973 oil prices jumped dramatically from $2.55 to nearly $15.00 a barrel. This enabled both Iran and Saudi Arabia to adopt ambitious and expensive development plans aimed at modernizing all aspects of their countries. Meanwhile both countries had also become more active in their political and economic foreign contacts.

Adding further momentum to the two countries' bilateral relationship was Saudi Crown Prince Fahd's visit to Iran in late 1975. The visit was in fact part of an official tour by the Crown Prince to Kuwait and Iraq. During his state visit to Iran, Prince Fahd conducted high-level talks which covered regional and international issues with the Shah and other Iranian officials.[94]

The Crown Prince's visit to Iran was further consolidated by King Khalid's visit to the Shah on 24 May 1976. Other high-ranking Saudi officials also exchanged visits with their Iranian counterparts: among them were Prince Sultan ibn Abd al-Aziz, Minister of Defence and Civil Aviation and Inspector-General, Prince Naif ibn Abd al-Aziz, Minister of the Interior,

Foreign Policy and Bilateral Foreign Relations 1932–82

Prince Saud al-Faisal, Minister of Foreign Affairs, and several other Saudi ministers. A number of high-ranking Iranian officials also visited the Kingdom and conducted important discussions with their Saudi counterparts: among them were Amir Abbas Hoveida (the Iranian Prime Minister), the Iranian Foreign Minister and the Iranian Oil Minister.

It would be fair to say that Shah Muhammad Riza Pahlavi was at this time in full agreement with Saudi Arabia's policies on a wide range of issues, in particular the need to: (a) maintain the security and stability of the Arabian/Persian Gulf region; (b) secure an overall settlement of the Arab–Israeli conflict and the restoration of Palestinian rights; (c) ensure an Israeli withdrawal from Jerusalem;[95] (d) promote Islamic solidarity among all Muslim nations and extend financial assistance to needy Islamic countries; (e) promote political, economic and military relations with the Western world, particularly the United States; and (f) combat communism and prevent its infiltration into the Islamic world, the Arab world and the African continent.

Such compliance with Saudi Arabia's policies underlined the Shah's responsibility for the policy of friendly relationships with the Kingdom and its leadership. However it was not until 1977 that the Shah agreed with Saudi Arabia's oil policies, particularly the price issue. During his November 1977 visit to the United States, the Shah extended a pledge to President Jimmy Carter that Iran would take a positive attitude in opposing any oil price increases at the forthcoming OPEC meetings.[96] Iran's new stance undoubtedly reinforced the longstanding Saudi position and helped offset opposition inside OPEC.

As early as 1978, however, the Shah began to feel the pressure of internal riots by the supporters of Ayatollah Khomeini and other opposition factions. For more than a year, the Shah had been contemplating a fundamental reorganization of the top government structure, replacing Iranian Court Minister Assadollah Alam,[97] who was suffering from leukaemia, by Prime Minister Hoveida. Hoveida himself was then replaced by Jamshid Amouzegar and other key positions were shuffled. The Shah's reorganization plans were primarily aimed at maintaining a balance between the different chief rivals within his government, maintenance of his supreme authority, calming the people and stopping the uprisings. The Shah was also practising the principle of 'centralized democracy', which in fact represented the theoretical basis of 'centralized bureaucracy', which in turn was practised by the socialist political systems.

By late 1978 the Shah's position inside Iran had weakened considerably. His reorganization efforts had failed and he was now alone, without

Saudi–Iranian Relations 1932–1982

competent advisers or strong political and military support. He was under additional daily strain as the world counted down to his 'zero hour'.

On 16 January 1979 the Shah left Iran for a vacation in Egypt, a country chosen so that he could keep a close eye on developments inside Iran. He was expecting a military coup to return him to power, as in 1953. In the event, he never saw his country again.

Saudi Arabia consistently reviewed internal developments in Iran, but never interfered in its internal affairs. The rise of Ayatollah Khomeini as the head of the Islamic Republic of Iran was a new phase in the modern history of Iran and ushered in a dramatic new era in Saudi–Iranian relations. (Chapter 4 will examine this relationship and post-revolutionary Iran from 1979 to 1982.)

Overall, Saudi–Iranian foreign policy and bilateral foreign relations from 1932 to 1979 were as good as could be expected. The two countries knew and worked with each other's strengths and weaknesses and their leaders had a good understanding of one another, particularly during the 1960s and 1970s. Misunderstandings as well as foreign-policy differences were handled carefully and settled peacefully. Even the obvious arrogance of Shah Muhammad Riza Pahlavi and his occasional political manoeuvres were wisely dealt with by the Saudi leadership, in line with Saudi Arabia's continuing policy of rationalism, realism and pragmatism.

Figure 1. State of Saudi–Iranian Relations, 1930–80

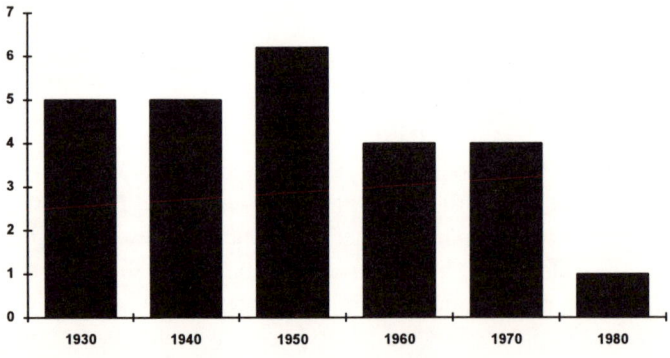

Good = 7, Normal = 6, Fluctuating = 4, Tense = 1

4
The Religious Relationship 1924–82

Religion has always been the most important element of human life; even in the most secular modern nation-states, its influence cannot be ignored. In the United States, for example, where separation of church and state has been in effect for 200 years, its coins bear the legend 'In God We Trust'; and in the Soviet Union, where every effort was made to stamp out religion, Islam, Christianity and Judaism are still very much alive. Even President Saddam Hussein of Iraq, when he saw the fortunes of war turn against him, abandoned the secular slogans of Arab Ba'thism and turned to the language and symbols of Islam. And governments that officially deny a deity greater than the state must still deal with the religious beliefs of the populace at an unofficial level.

Religion has played a particularly crucial role in the lives of the people of the Middle East. The region is the birthplace of the three monotheistic religions, Judaism, Christianity and Islam. All the prophets and holy messengers through whom almighty Allah (God) revealed himself, starting with Noah and ending with Muhammad, were born of that region. Holy shrines of the three religions are located throughout the Middle East, the most important being in Jerusalem, Makkah and Madinah.

Islam, Christianity and Judaism have all played a major role in the development of Middle Eastern, and indeed world, civilization. Judaism's contribution has been both in its influence on the subsequent development of Christian and Islamic religious thought and in the cultural attainments of its small but worldwide population. Christianity is the basis of Western civilization. Middle Eastern culture, on the other hand, is virtually indistinguishable from Islamic culture, whose impact stretches far beyond, from Indonesia in East Asia to Mauritania in West Africa. Thus these three monotheistic religions are an indelible part of the fabric of world civilization.

In the Middle East, Islamic history and values have so permeated the culture that it is impossible to talk rationally about one without talking about the other. Islam is more than a religion, it is a total way of life, a complete cosmic system. Universal in concept, it not only binds together into a single faith 800 million Muslims throughout the world, but it also binds together the polyglot national, ethnic and religious groups of the Middle East into a single culture.

Since Islam developed into the dominant world religion in the seventh century, the political fortunes of Muslim rulers have waxed and waned. In the words of an Islamic proverb, 'Nothing remains for ever, except the face of almighty Allah.' Thus the mighty empires of the Arabs, Persians, Moguls and Turks have all disappeared and the locus of contemporary political power has shifted away from the Muslim world to the industrialized states of America, Europe and Japan.

This chapter will discuss the religious relationship between Saudi Arabia and Iran. Despite the universal qualities of Islamic Middle East culture and the tendency of Westerners to stereotype all Middle Eastern peoples as essentially the same, there are major differences between the peoples of the Middle East, even between Muslim communities. Nowhere is this difference more evident than between the predominantly Sunni Muslim Arabs of Saudi Arabia and the predominantly Shi'a Muslim Persians of present-day Iran.

Understanding Islam

Islam is a monotheistic religion that originated in the Arabian peninsula. In AD 610 the Arab prophet Muhammad ibn Abdallah (Peace be upon him) was called upon by almighty Allah to propagate and preach for Islam, which is a universal religion and open to all who believe its tenets. Today, more than 800 million Muslims all over the world accept the religion of one almighty Allah, commonly known as the doctrine of *tawheed*. 'Islam' is an Arabic word meaning simply 'submission and obedience'. Therefore the religion stands for total submission and obedience to Allah.

Islam is based on five major pillars:
1. There is no God but Allah and Muhammad is his messenger (*shahadah*).
2. The performance of *salat* (prayer).

3. The payment of *zakat* (tax).
4. Fasting of Ramadan (*sawm*).
5. Making the pilgrimage (*hajj*), which is only obligatory for those who can physically and financially afford it.

In essence, anyone who believes in the five major pillars of Islam is a Muslim. Other concepts, beliefs and interpretations of Islamic laws and regulations come after these five pillars. For example, there are today two major Islamic sects: Sunnis, who make up 90 per cent of the Muslim population; and Shi'a, whose adherents comprise the remaining 10 per cent of the Muslim world. These two sects differ in a number of Islamic practices and interpretations of worship, laws and beliefs. However, the five pillars of Islam apply equally to both sects and no differences exist in this regard between them.

In the area of Islamic law, or *Shari'a*, there are two primary sources of doctrine and practice: the holy Quran, which was revealed to the Prophet Muhammad; and the *Sunna*, which is the example or model of the Prophet. The *Sunna* interprets and explains the teachings of the holy Quran. Islamic jurisprudence is entirely based on these two major sources of Islamic law. Unlike other written laws, the *Shari'a* is the path laid down by almighty Allah and is a framework for all human actions and undertakings. Muslims all over the world are obliged to follow this path without deviating from it.

A third important source of doctrine and justice is *Ijma'*, or unanimity of opinion. The practice of *Ijma'* is conducted by a group of knowledgeable people who assemble to deliberate an issue in light of the Quran and the available tradition. The usefulness of *Ijma'* depends on the firm conviction that truth is absolute and ascertainable and that knowledgeable people cannot deviate from the two primary sources of Islamic law.

Since the death of the Prophet Muhammad, and with the expansion of Islam to new territories, the two primary sources of Islamic jurisprudence have remained the same. A number of Islamic jurists, researchers and scholars—known in Islam as *alims*—have emerged and been instrumental in shaping the policies of Islamic law in accordance with new situations that have arisen. Among those jurists were four prominent Sunni Imams who had their own schools of Islamic teaching. Their Islamic work and research attracted a broad base of Sunni Muslims who later became the followers of those Imams' paths, or *madhhab*.

Under the current system of Sunni Islam, there are four duly recognized schools of Sunni Islamic teachings: the Hanafi school, named after its founder, Imam Abu Hanifa No'man ibn Sabit (AD 699-767); the Maliki school, named after its founder, Imam Malik ibn Anas al-Arabi (AD 713–95); the Shafa'i school, named after its founder, Imam Muhammad ibn Idris al-Shafa'i (AD 767–819); and the Hanbali school, named after its founder, Imam Abu Abdallah Ahmad ibn Hanbal (AD 780–855).[1] These four schools have not adopted new sources or changed the basic two primary sources of Islamic *Shari'a*. On the contrary, they have adhered strictly to these two major sources. Subsequently, they have succeeded in contributing significantly to the advancement of the science of Islamic law and in developing theories on various legal concepts. Today's *Shari'a* is a dynamic system that is neither too rigid nor too flexible.[2]

Meanwhile, there are four basic concepts of Islam, which go hand-in-hand with the five major pillars. These four concepts are:

1. The concept of *tawheed*, the truthful belief that there is no God but almighty Allah who is the sole creator of the universe.
2. The concept of *imam*, the truthful belief in the existence of Allah, His angels, His holy books, His prophets, destiny (*qadar*) whether it is good or bad, and *al-yawm al-akhira* (the Day of Judgement).
3. The concept of *ihsan*, the worship of Allah as if you can see Him; but if you do not see Him, He sees you.
4. The concept of *ibadah* (worship), worshipping Allah alone in accordance with His orders, and by all pure and good means.

Contrary to the Western perception, Islam is a united religion. It cannot be divided into categories, such as Sunni Islam or Shi'a Islam. It is united in a way that binds all Muslims, whether Sunnis or Shi'a, under one banner. From the Sunni viewpoint, the Shi'a have deviated from the Sunni path, and have chosen their own path and version of Islamic traditions and practices.

Shi'ism came into existence after the death of the Prophet Muhammad. It is not a second branch of Islam because Islam is one and cannot be divided. Shi'ism derives its name from the Arabic word *shi'a*, which means 'followers'. In this respect, believers in Shi'ism follow the fourth Islamic Caliph, Ali ibn Abi Talib, who was also the Prophet Muhammad's cousin and son-in-law. The Shi'a believe that Ali was supposed to succeed the Prophet immediately upon his death and become the first Caliph of Islam. They also believe that the correct line of succession was to be through the descendants of Ali and his wife Fatima, the Prophet's daughter.[3] Their belief was further strengthened and their position hardened when Ali was assassinated (in 40 AH/AD 672) and his son Hussein met a violent death. Thus the Shi'a considered Hussein as the rightful successor to Ali, and denied the Omayyads' claim to the Caliphate under Mo'awiyah ibn Abi Sufyan. They also objected to the Omayyads' moving the Caliphate from Madinah to Damascus.

In later centuries, the Shi'a divided into three different sects, the Twelvers, the Zaydis and the Isma'ilis.[4] The Twelvers believe in twelve Imams, with Ali as the First Imam, his son Hassan as Second, his son Hussein as Third, until the Twelfth Imam Muhammad al-Muntazar, 'the awaited one'. In this connection, the present-day Shi'a in Iran are Twelvers. The Zaydis are the followers of Imam Zayd, who stood against the Omayyad Caliph in the eighth century. Today, they are based in North Yemen and are considered the closest Shi'a branch to the Sunnis in matters of jurisprudence and tradition. The Isma'ilis believe in only seven Imams and they are known as 'the Seveners'. They emerged as a separate Shi'a sect during the tenth century. Their present recognized spiritual and secular leader is Prince Agha Khan. Nowadays, the majority live in Pakistan.

Like the Sunnis, the Twelver Shi'a have their own schools of thought. As might be expected, their jurists and scholars have interpreted the *Shari'a* in accordance with their own beliefs and have not entirely adhered to the two major and primary sources of Islamic law. This stems from their belief that the Prophet Muhammad died before finishing his message.[5] They therefore hold that it is the duty of the *mujtahids* (jurists and scholars) to complete that task under the guidance of a Shi'a Imam.

There are three well-known schools of thought in Twelver Shi'ism. The Usulis or Mujtahids believe they are supposed to choose a living *mujtahid*, or Imam, to interpret Islamic laws and doctrines. Consequently, they obey him and abide by his judgements. The Akhbaris are followers of traditions, and the practices of the Prophet Muhammad and his Caliphs. In this sense, they see no need for *mujtahids* or interpreters. The Mu'tazilites adhere to a moderate, rational theological outlook.[6]

While the Shi'a do not differ from the Sunnis on the major five pillars of Islam, there are differences over many areas relating to Islamic law and its interpretation. Moreover, whereas the Sunnis believe that the order of succession after the death of the Prophet Muhammad was right and legal, the Shi'a deny it and consider it illegal. Furthermore, whereas the Shi'a believe in the need for a recognized learned Imam (*alim*) who can lead the Muslim *ummah* and guide it, the Sunnis do not accept this necessity.

As a universal and united religion, Islam has a number of important moral precepts and characteristics that mean that it can be practised in and applied to any society at any time. These characteristics are as follows:

1. *Equality*. All believers are equal in the eyes of almighty Allah. However, those who are more pious are the more blessed.
2. *Justice*. Islam is the religion of justice. Believers from all walks of life have rights as well as duties. They are obliged not to wrong or harm fellow members of the community, whether Muslims or non-Muslims.
3. *Freedom*. All people are created free by almighty Allah and no one has the right to treat them as slaves.
4. *Peace*. Islam is the religion of peace and harmony. Consequently, all societies are deemed to live in peace and harmony. Brotherhood among all believers should be maintained and truthfully practised.

In the final analysis, it could be said that Islam is a universal religion. It is the religion of equality, justice, freedom and peace. Moreover, it does not contradict the other heavenly religions. On the contrary, it recognizes those religions and their respective tenets revealed to the prophets.

Saudi Arabia and Islam

The Kingdom of Saudi Arabia has embraced Islam as its state religion since the Kingdom's founding in September 1932. The Kingdom encompasses the heartland of Islam and is the custodian of the two holy mosques, Makkah and Madinah. Its present monarch holds the title of 'The Custodian of the Two Holy Mosques'. Today, Makkah is regarded as the most sacred shrine and the holiest place on earth for the more than 800 million Muslims. Muslims who are able, physically and financially, are required to perform the *hajj* in Makkah at least once during their lifetime. The fifth pillar of Islam, the *hajj*, is performed annually according to the lunar calendar. During the pilgrimage, Muslims from all over the world and from all walks of life gather in Makkah and its surrounding religious places for four consecutive days. There they seek almighty Allah's blessings and mercy.

The Prophet Muhammad's mosque, regarded as the second holiest place on earth for all Muslims, is located in the heart of Madinah city proper and is the centre around which the whole city was built and planned.[7] The mosque was originally built by the Prophet himself upon his migration from Makkah.

The Islamic nature of modern Saudi Arabia is further embodied in the Kingdom's choice of national flag, which is a green rectangle with, at its centre, written in white lettering, the creed, or *shahadah*, which is the cornerstone of Islam: 'There is no God but Allah, and Muhammad is the messenger of Allah.' Beneath it is an unsheathed sword lying parallel to the

The Religious Relationship 1924–82

shahadah. Out of respect for the *shahadah* inscribed on it,[8] it is against the law to fly the Saudi flag at half-mast or allow it to touch the ground or water.

To emphasize further its unique Islamic nature, the Kingdom of Saudi Arabia has adopted the holy Quran as its constitution. The Quran was revealed by almighty Allah to his messenger and Prophet Muhammad. Therefore, it is divine and nothing like it can be composed by a human mind. In addition, the Quran is the first source of Islamic law. Combined with the *Sunna*, the Quran embodies all laws and regulations that govern every aspect of human activity and worship. Hence, all Saudi laws and regulations, whether religious or secular, must comply with the Islamic *Shari'a*. In this sense, Saudi Arabia is unique among other Islamic countries in its adherence to Islamic *Shari'a* as the only basis for all its laws and actions.

The Kingdom of Saudi Arabia is sometimes referred to as the 'Wahhabi' state, after Sheikh Muhammad ibn Abd al-Wahhab, who was born in Oyaynah north of al-Dar'iyah, the home of the Al Sauds since 1703.[9] The Sheikh was raised in a family of religious scholars following the Hanbali school of Islamic law. Throughout his education, he was influenced by the ideas and teachings of Sheikh Ibn Taymiyya, a theologian and jurist who died in 1328.[10] In 1745 Sheikh Muhammad ibn Abd al-Wahhab settled in the Saudi emirate of al-Dar'iyah. There, he was received warmly by its ruler Muhammad ibn Saud and both men joined hands in expanding Saudi political power on a religious basis. By 1773 Saudi power and authority had extended over all of Najd, including the emirate of Riyadh. Consequently, Wahhabism and its religious teachings spread with Saudi political power. In 1765 a Saudi–Wahhabi military force took control of Makkah, the most sacred city of Islam, and two years later Madinah was captured. This development brought the Saudi state into direct confrontation with the Ottoman Empire, whose Sultan considered himself the Caliph of all Muslims and guardian of the holy shrines. In 1811 the Ottoman Sultan ordered his *wali* (governor) in Egypt, Muhammad Ali Pasha, to send an expedition to the Hijaz in order to regain control of the two holy cities. Outnumbered and ill-equipped, the Saudi–Wahhabi force had to conclude a truce with Muhammad Ali Pasha's son Tusan, who led the Egyptian expedition, ceding control of the two holy cities in 1814.

But the Saudi–Wahhabi religious movement to serve the two holy shrines did not end. In 1912 King Abd al-Aziz ibn Saud, after settling his power base in Riyadh, united and organized the tribes of Arabia into a religious brotherhood movement that later became known as the Ikhwan movement, or Muwahideen. The basic aim of the movement was to spread the orthodox teachings of Islam under the banner of Wahhabism. From there, King Abd al-Aziz (then Sultan of Najd and its Dependencies) began his struggle to regain the two holy cities of Islam. During the period between 1924 and 1926, he conquered the Hijaz and gained full control over the two holy cities, Makkah and Madinah, which continues today.

Serving the two holy shrines is an Islamic honour for the Kingdom of Saudi Arabia, its leaders and its people. It is also a great responsibility towards almighty Allah and the Muslim *ummah* that the Kingdom takes very seriously. One of the responsibilities involves attending to the needs of the approximately 2 million *hajjis* who make the pilgrimage every year. They arrive and leave within a very limited time-frame. The Kingdom has nevertheless handled the pilgrimage season competently since 1925. In addition, the country's leadership continues to put great effort and funds into expanding the capacity of the two holy shrines in order to accommodate the ever-increasing numbers of pilgrims and visitors and to extend the facilities.

At its creation as a fully independent and sovereign state in September 1932, the Kingdom of Saudi Arabia pronounced that Islam was the state religion, the Quran was its constitution and Islamic *Shari'a* was its law. This is a unique situation for a twentieth-century political entity and one of which the Kingdom, its leadership and its population are proud. The Saudi population, estimated at 12 million today, are all Muslims. Moreover, the Saudi calendar year (known as the *hijra* calendar) is based on the date of the Prophet Muhammad's migration from the holy city of Makkah to Madinah. Today, the Kingdom of Saudi Arabia is probably the only Islamic country to use the *hijra* calendar.

Iran and Islam

Within six years of his migration from Makkah to Madinah in AD 628, the Prophet Muhammad sent messengers to kings, emperors and princes of other nations, calling on them to accept and embrace Islam. This task emanated from the fact that Muhammad viewed himself as a universal Prophet sent to all people without regard to race, colour or religion.

Among those kings and emperors was Chosroes, the Emperor of Persia. Persia at that time was one of the two superpowers which shared power and influence over much of the region.[11] When Chosroes received the Prophet Muhammad's message calling on him to embrace Islam, he was shocked and reacted angrily. He tore up the Prophet's letter and asked his ally, the King of Yemen, to send him the head of the Prophet. During this time, Chosroes died and was succeeded by his son Cyrus. Consequently, the Persian Empire started to wane and lose many of its predominantly Arab territories although Persia itself remained intact until the reign of the first Caliph, Abu Bakr (AD 632–34.).

In 634 Omar ibn al-Khattab, the second Muslim Caliph, succeeded Abu Bakr. He issued orders to the commanders of the Muslim armies to conquer a number of territories including the remaining part of mainland Persia. By the year 645 those armies had conquered Damascus and Jerusalem, Egypt and Libya, which had been under Roman rule, as well as the rest of Persia.[12] At the time, Persia was divided between paganism and Zoroastrianism.[13] Both ideologies were declining, however, despite the influence of the clergy. Thus the Persians were in need of a stronger faith and ideology and, in essence, Islam appealed to them. Indeed, they embraced the new religion readily and converted to it without much hesitation. Following the advent of Islam into Persia, the whole Persian Empire came under the rule of the Sunni Caliphate, and Persians from all walks of life practised the Sunni path of Islam. The ensuing years witnessed the flourishing of Islam inside Persia and the contribution of Persian scientists and artists to the glory of Islam.

It was not until the crumbling of the Safavid Empire during the seventeenth century that the theory of Twelver Shi'ism became widespread, creating a new class in Persian society, the religious class. The members of this class, who have become known as mullahs, wanted a leading role in the society. A few years later they were able to achieve their goal and began to exert influence on Persian society as a whole. Their influence and power encompassed both the spiritual and the political life of the country.

After the downfall of the Safavids in the early eighteenth century, Persia came under the rule of the Qajars. The Qajari Shahs none the less had to respect the powerful mullahs in order to avoid any confrontation with them. However, this cordial relationship between the Qajari Shahs and the mullahs was interrupted during the reign of Nadir (Nasser al-Din) Shah (1848–96), who limited the mullahs' power and influence.[14] But with his assassination on 1 May 1896, the mullahs reasserted themselves and took advantage of the weakness of his successor to regain their lost influence, including the supervision of educational institutions and the restoration of their financial privileges. At the same time, their political activities increased. The mullahs' power and influence continued to grow until 1911 when both the British and the Russians began to intervene in the country's affairs.

With the outbreak of the First World War, the role of the mullahs, particularly in the political affairs of Persia, began a brief decline. In 1921 Riza Khan (later Riza Shah Pahlavi) considered returning Persia to its ancient religion, but decided not to out of fear of a confrontation with the mullahs. Instead, he chose to incorporate them into the political arena in order to win their support and to guarantee his succession to power with their blessing. Indeed, in 1925, and with the mullahs' backing, he deposed the last Qajari Shah and the following year he had himself crowned the Shah-en-Shah (King of Kings) of Iran.[15]

The relationship between Riza Shah and the mullahs did not last long. To the Shah, the mullahs represented a backward class inside Iranian society and he wanted to curb their power. Therefore, he moved against them and limited their traditional power in the fields of law, education and religious endowments.[16] This resulted in open confrontation, and the mullahs were only too pleased to see Riza Shah abdicate in 1941 in favour of his son, Shah Muhammad Riza Pahlavi.

The new young Shah followed the path laid by his father. In order to strengthen his control over Iran, he needed the mullahs' support. This led him to develop cordial relations with them. Moreover, he issued a number of proclamations upholding traditional Islamic culture and practices. Subsequently, he won the mullahs' support during the Mossadeq crisis of 1953. Furthermore, with the mullahs' co-operation and support, he was able to crush the communists in 1954.

The mid-1940s witnessed the rise of a number of politically oriented Islamic organizations such as the Mojahedin-e Islam and the Fedaiyan-e Islam. These organizations, along with independent mullahs, began in the mid-1950s to oppose the Shah's internal policies and to question his external alliances with the Western powers, including the United States. The result was an unavoidable confrontation between the Shah and the religious establishment. In order to win his battle with the mullahs, the Shah moved fast to concentrate all powers in himself. To accomplish this, he first launched a crackdown on all newly established Islamic organizations. Second, he sent many of the leading mullahs into exile. Third, he announced land reform programmes to win the support of the rural population. Fourth, he created a police type of an intelligence service, the SAVAK.[17] By the late 1950s and early 1960s, he had become an absolute monarch who could disregard the demands of the religious class: he had crushed their power.

The Shah believed that he had dealt with the mullahs once and for all. But he was quite mistaken and by 1977 the mullahs' underground activities surfaced again and a wide range of Iranians expressed their outrage openly in the streets of Tehran and other major cities. The Shah panicked, and his ill-advised tactics in dealing with the situation contributed to the deterioration of his position in the eyes of his people. The mullahs took full advantage of the situation by putting continuous pressure on him until they forced him to leave the country.

The Religious Relationship 1924-82

As early as January 1979 it was clear that the mullahs had won their battle with the Shah and had Iran to themselves. On 1 February 1979 Imam Ayatollah Ruhollah Khomeini, the spiritual leader of the Iranian revolution, and his entourage of clergymen landed at Tehran airport in a chartered aeroplane from Paris. He immediately announced the end of the monarchy and the establishment of an Islamic Republic.

Saudi Arabia, Iran and Islam

The relationship between Iran and Saudi Arabia during the period 1924-79 was very cordial compared to the atmosphere following the 1979 revolution. This cordiality was based on three factors. First, Saudi Arabia and Iran severed diplomatic relations only once in more than five decades of their bilateral relations as a result of a religious dispute, and then it was brief. Second, the leadership in both countries was willing to solve the religious disputes peacefully. And third, the lack of a strong Islamic adherence on the part of Iran's Shahs resulted in the two countries having a quiet, if not cordial, religious relationship from 1924 to 1979.

In 1924 King Abd al-Aziz (then Sultan of Najd and its Dependencies) took Makkah and restored his family's control over this Islamic holy shrine. Two years later, he succeeded in taking Madinah.[18] As a result, many Muslim nations expressed their concern over the safety of these two holy shrines. The reason behind this concern was attributed to the spread of some false rumours claiming that the Saudi military forces had damaged the shrines. Among the Muslim countries which expressed their concern were Iran, under Riza Shah Pahlavi, and Egypt, under King Fouad, a descendant cf Muhammad Ali Pasha.

For his part, King Abd al-Aziz denied the rumours and announced that an investigation of the two holy shrines by any Muslim country was welcome. In addition, the King declared that he did not intend to proclaim himself as the Caliph of the Muslim *ummah*. He further acknowledged that the two holy shrines were of such great importance to all Muslim nations that he planned to hold an Islamic Conference whereby all Muslims could meet and discuss the future of the two holy cities. Such assurances calmed the concerns of the Islamic community around the world and made it possible for the King to proceed in his plans to promote the holy shrines and secure access to them.[19]

In an attempt to please his Shi'a clergymen and secure their support for his own political future in Persia, Riza Khan (later Riza Shah Pahlavi) was the first Muslim leader to respond to King Abd al-Aziz's announcements. He sent two Persian teams to the Hijaz to investigate the situation inside the holy shrines to verify the rumours of damage. Riza Khan was known not to be a religious man, yet he did not mind using religion to achieve his political secular goals. Further, he believed strongly in the concept of separation of power between politics and religion. However, he did not want to lose control over the religious establishment and, therefore, the investigation offer idea appealed very much to him.

The first investigative delegation was assigned to visit Makkah and report back to the Persian government on its findings. The delegates were also instructed to prepare the groundwork for the visit of a second delegation to Madinah. On 21 October 1925 the first delegation arrived in Jeddah; it consisted of two prominent Persian diplomats, the Persian Minister to Egypt and the Persian Consul-General in Palestine. Upon their arrival, they were received cordially by King Abd al-Aziz on the outskirts of the city. He provided his own cars for their journey to Makkah, as well as the services of his aides to facilitate the mission.[20] Meanwhile, he welcomed any other Muslim delegations wanting to investigate the situation inside the holy shrines.

The Persian delegation was interested in investigating the condition of the Great Mosque, and the tombs of the Prophet Muhammad's companions and other leading Muslim scholars (*alims*). With regard to the Great Mosque, the delegation was pleased to see that no damage had occurred to the Mosque or to the Ka'bah itself.[21] Concerning the tombs of the Prophet and his followers, the delegation was unaware that most of the companions were buried in Madinah and not in Makkah. Even those buried in Makkah had no domes on their graves. Upon its return to Jeddah, the delegation did not ask for another meeting with King Abd al-Aziz, but expressed its satisfaction with what it had seen. In fact, the members concluded that the holy shrines in Makkah, under the rule of King Abd al-Aziz, were in much better condition than they had been under the rule of the Hashimite Kings when the safety and the overall condition of the shrines had been vulnerable and uncertain. In 1921, for example, when the Hashimites had been unable to secure the routes to the holy places in Makkah and Madinah and organize the *hajj*, they had cancelled the *hajj* season entirely and prevented Muslims from making the pilgrimage that year.[22]

The second Persian delegation actually arrived in Jeddah before the first, on 20 October 1925. It did not ask to see King Abd al-Aziz and waited in Jeddah for the arrival of the first delegation. After the first delegation's meeting with the King, the second delegation proceeded to Madinah. It was composed of the Persian Consul to Damascus and an aide. They were driven to Makkah and from there to Madinah. Like their fellow Persians, their priority was to investigate the condition of the Prophet's mosque and the tombs of his companions and other *alims*.

Upon its return from Madinah, this second Persian delegation made no comment to the Saudi officials but looked very disheartened. It was clear that the delegates did not like the Saudi-Wahhabi destruction of the domes built on the tombs of the companions of the Prophet and the early Islamic scholars. However, they were pleased to see that the Prophet's tomb itself and the dome on it were unscathed. From the Saudi-Wahhabi point of view, the veneration and the building of domes on the tombs of the Prophet's companions or holy religious men is considered a desecration of the worship of Allah alone. Thus, even the graveyard of Sheikh Muhammad ibn Abd al-Wahhab, the founder of the Wahhabi movement, and those of the Saudi Kings are not marked. This tradition complies with the Hanbali school of thought and is aimed at dissuading Muslims from seeking the *baraka* (blessings) of those holy men, an act which is contrary to orthodox Islamic teachings. None the less, visiting the tombs is not forbidden or prohibited in Islam.

After the completion of their missions in Makkah and Madinah, the two Persian delegations left the Hijaz separately and returned home. The fact that Riza Shah did not correspond further with King Abd al-Aziz regarding this matter suggests that he was satisfied with his delegations' reports and was not critical of the Saudi actions. Moreover, his sending of a Persian delegation to attend the first Islamic Conference in Makkah in 1926 implied that he had decided to put behind him the issue of the domed tombs.

King Abd al-Aziz's call for an Islamic Conference was undoubtedly a brilliant idea. Through that call, the King wanted to reassure the Muslim *ummah* that he sought to maintain good and constructive religious relationships with all Muslim nations and their leaders and he disregarded all sectarian religious differences among the Muslim *ummah*. Moreover, he made it clear to the Muslim leaders that his concern was to unify the Muslim nations and to serve and safeguard the two holy shrines. Therefore, his invitation to the conference was extended to all Muslim leaders, including those of Persia. On 22 January 1926 the King made a formal statement of his good intentions and pointed out that there had been almost no response from Muslim leaders to his call for an Islamic Conference to discuss the situation and status of the holy places in the Hijaz region. In that statement the King said, '...So, as I find that the Islamic world is not concerned about this important matter, I have granted them [the people of the Hijaz] the freedom to decide what they will.'[23]

Abd al-Aziz's statement certainly had an effect on the Muslim world leaders, particularly after the people of the Hijaz extended their *bay'ah* (allegiance) to the King. During the *hajj* season of 1926, the first Islamic Conference was held in Makkah and all Muslim nations, including Persia, were represented except for Egypt. During that *hajj* season approximately 191,000 pilgrims came to perform their pilgrimage, an eightfold increase over the previous year.[24]

The delegates who attended the conference debated freely on a wide variety of religious topics without focusing on the underlying political issue of running the Hijaz region. However, the idea of creating a pan-Islamic organization was briefly discussed as well as the issue of the financial requirements and needs for maintaining and serving the two holy places. Since no Islamic country, including Iran, was willing to commit itself to financial support of the holy shrines, and in keeping with his previous promises of serving the two holy cities, King Abd al-Aziz agreed to take on the financial responsibility of maintaining the shrines. This commitment was given by the King despite the fact that his newly created country was itself in need of financial assistance.

As a result of this first Islamic Conference, it was clear that King Abd al-Aziz had won the Islamic world's *bay'ah* for his right to serve, maintain and supervise the shrines. This also meant that he was solely responsible for securing the routes to the holy cities for all Muslim visitors to the holy land and for enlarging the shrines as needed for the continuing growth of the *hajj*. King Abd al-Aziz lived up to his responsibility and the routes to the holy shrines were secured and made safe. And every Saudi King since has made sure the routes to the holy cities of Makkah and Madinah are safe and secure for the millions of Muslims coming from all over the world who today make the *hajj*.

Differences in the Practice of Islam

Although the *hajj* has remained an important aspect of the religious ties and relationships between Saudi Arabia and Iran, as in every kind of bilateral relationship, the religious ties between the two countries have their differences. These differences lie in a number of religious beliefs and practices, including the way the *hajj* and the *salat* (daily prayers) are performed, and many other Islamic practices. The following discussion will focus on the most controversial issues.

The Grand Pilgrimage (Hajj)
As mentioned earlier, the *hajj* is the fifth pillar of Islam and is one of the most important religious issues between the Kingdom of Saudi Arabia and

Iran, as well as the whole Islamic world. In *The Hajj Today*, Dr David E. Long describes the Saudi responsibility during the annual *hajj* season as follows:

> Nearly every agency of the Saudi government becomes involved, either in regulating the privately operated *hajj* service industry, or in providing direct administrative services. Such a task would tax the most sophisticated government bureaucracy, and yet Saudi Arabia, where public administration is still in a developing stage, manages to get the job done each year.[25]

The *hajj* remains one of the most crucial issues in the Saudi-Iranian religious relationship. During the reign of Riza Pahlavi (1925–41), Iranians were discouraged from making the pilgrimage or visiting the holy places in the Hijaz region. Iranians who wanted to make their *hajj* needed special permission from the Iranian government. During this period, Iranian passports carried the statement, 'The bearer of this passport is allowed to visit everywhere but the Hijaz.'[26] After the fall of Riza Pahlavi in 1941, Iranian *hajjis* (pilgrims) began to visit the holy shrines in Makkah and Madinah to make their pilgrimage. Moreover, modern transport systems and highways constructed by the Saudi government have made it possible for Iranians and other Muslim believers to make the pilgrimage in greater numbers.

The total Grand Pilgrimage of 1987 was 1,800,000 *hajjis*, in comparison with 232,971 in 1954. These figures include the locals, of whom many are from different Muslim countries either residing or working in the Kingdom of Saudi Arabia. Table 3 shows the number of Iranian pilgrims who made the *hajj* between 1961 and 1987.[27]

These figures clearly indicate the steady rise in the numbers of Iranian pilgrims since the Iranian revolution in 1979. At the same time, the table shows that the number of pilgrims fluctuated during the 1960s. In 1966 the total number was 35,334 *hajjis*, but in 1967 it dropped to 22,903. This particular decrease is directly related to the political situation in the Middle East at the time. Because of the Arab-Israeli war in 1967, many Iranians decided not to make their pilgrimage. Fewer pilgrims came from other parts of the world that year, as well.

The enormous increase in Iranians making the *hajj* since 1987 was not the result of individual Iranians' desire to make the *hajj* but of the Iranian government's insisting on sending as many pilgrims as it desired. This action by the Iranians placed enormous pressure on the overall capacity of the

Table 3. No. of Iranian Pilgrims who Made the Hajj, 1961–87

Year	No.	Year	No.
1961	12,000	1975	n/a
1962	11,000	1976	n/a
1963	17,000	1977	n/a
1964	19,073	1978	n/a
1965	24,937	1979	n/a
1966	35,334	1980	10,539
1967	22,903	1981	75,391
1968	13,642	1982	89,503
1969	15,132	1983	103,044
1970	48,368	1984	154,958
1971	30,299	1985	152,227
1972	45,298	1986	152,149
1973	57,230	1987	157,395
1974	57,314		

facilities available for the pilgrims and was a disservice to all Muslims throughout the world. In response to this situation, the Saudi Arabian government brought this situation to the attention of the Foreign Ministers of the Islamic world during its 1988 Summit in Amman. In accordance with a resolution passed by this body, the Saudi government now demands that Iran send no more than 10 per cent of its total population.[28] This resolution was passed due to the fact that the two holy shrines obviously cannot obsorb the ever-increasing numbers of Muslims wishing to make the pilgrimage.

Nevertheless, this kind of tension over the Grand Pilgrimage between Saudi Arabia and Iran is not new and, historically, there have been a number of different types of incidents. During the 1943 pilgrimage season, two incidents occurred. In the first, an Iranian pilgrimage caravan, heading towards Makkah, had to camp near a small village in the Najd area. At dawn, the caravan prayer caller (*mu'adhin*) began to call for the morning prayer (*fajr*) in the traditional Shi'a call for prayer (*adhan*), which is different from the Sunni call. He was heard by some of the village's inhabitants, who came to the Iranian camp and started arguing with the Iranian pilgrims. The argument led to a hand-to-hand fight and the local police had to intervene. No casualties were recorded and on the same day the caravan continued on its way to Makkah. In the second incident, the Saudi religious police arrested an Iranian pilgrim (Hajji Abu Talib al-Yazdi) inside the Great Mosque in Makkah for throwing excrement at the Ka'bah. He was arrested, tried, found guilty and beheaded in accordance with the *Shari'a*.[29]

From the Iranian point of view, the two incidents were linked and the government protested vehemently at the execution of the pilgrim. After a tense exchange of official letters between the Saudi and Iranian governments, Iran decided in March 1944 to sever its diplomatic relations with Saudi Arabia. Such incidents, which are not unusual during the pilgrimage season, indicate how delicate the Saudi-Iranian religious relationship was at the time.

Six years later, during the pilgrimage season of 1949, the religious leader of the Iranian pilgrimage mission to Makkah, Ayatollah Kashani, issued a *fatwa* that the date of standing at Arafat—the most important day in making the *hajj*—was recorded incorrectly by the Saudi authorities and that he and his Iranian pilgrims would not leave Arafat at the end of the day, as all pilgrims are required. Learning of this, King Abd al-Aziz, wanting to avoid a disturbance and chaos among the pilgrims of other Muslim nations, sent three of his closest aides to talk to Ayatollah Kashani and try to convince him to leave Arafat along with the rest of the Iranian pilgrims at the specified time. Further, he instructed his aides to make it clear to Kashani that if he and his followers did not leave peacefully, the King would have no choice but to take tough measures and force them to leave. This action was successful and no force was needed as the Iranians left at the appointed time. Fortunately, another very serious crisis between the two countries was avoided.[30]

During the 1962 pilgrimage season, some Iranian pilgrims in Madinah tried to throw dirt inside the tomb of the Prophet Muhammad. The act was not directed at the Prophet himself, however, but at the first two Caliphs of Islam, Abu Bakr and Omar, who are buried with him in the same tomb. The Shi'a's hatred of the Prophet's first three Caliphs is well known, since they believe that the fourth Caliph, Ali, deserved to be the successor of the Prophet. None the less, these pilgrims were seen by the Saudi religious police and a fight broke out between the Iranian pilgrims and a number of local citizens. Although no one was killed in the fight, a number of Iranians as well as local citizens were taken to the nearby hospital suffering from serious injuries.[31]

In 1967 a dispute arose between Saudi Arabian Airlines and Iran Air over the transportation of Iranian pilgrims. This was resolved by an agreement that Iran Air would transport the Iranian pilgrims and that the Saudi airline would charge 15 per cent of the ticket price for handling and servicing the Iranian pilgrims' flights.

These incidents demonstrate that the Iranian pilgrims tend to create, whether intentionally or not, some problems during the annual *hajj*. Indeed, it would seem that they try to antagonize the Saudi authorities and Sunni Muslims; their visits to the tombs of the Prophet's companions at the Baqi' graveyard in Madinah are always accompanied by unlawful behaviour. The Saudi government tries to disregard the Iranian misconduct, but it intercedes when these activities exceed the bounds of appropriate behaviour.

Prayer (Salat) *and Other Religious Issues*
Differences in prayer (*salat*) are another crucial issue in the religious relationship between Saudi Arabia and Iran. According to Iranian Shi'a practices, collective prayer behind a Sunni Imam is not acceptable behaviour. Therefore, during the annual pilgrimage, the Iranian pilgrims do not follow the Sunni Imams of the two holy mosques in Makkah and Madinah.[32] Moreover, when they prostrate themselves in prayer, they place a piece of clay, which is brought from Karbala (Iraq), on the ground and put their foreheads on it; and unlike Sunnis, who pray five times a day, the Shi'a, including Iranians, pray only three times a day. These differences between Sunni and Shi'a religious practices occasionally result in clashes with Saudi Sunni locals, Sunni pilgrims from different Islamic nations and the Iranians.

In reality, there are countless religious ideological differences between the Sunnis and the Shi'a, but it would not serve our purpose to go into more detail. Suffice it to say that these differences are responsible for the deterioration of the religious relationship between Saudi Arabia and Iran. Consequently, such situations tend to lend themselves to political misunderstandings, which may lead to political crises.

It is important to realize that these situations, when they arise, are not just Iranian-Saudi related incidents, but an attitude of the Iranians who, after having toppled the Shah of Iran in 1979, wish to escalate their activities, particularly during the *hajj* season, by creating unseemly incidents ranging from religious demonstrations and politically oriented marches, to the distribution of pamphlets. Such acts are direct actions designed to politicize the pilgrimage.

Further, they have brought with them to the holy shrines quantities of drugs such as opium, which they use regularly and consider legal. This is in direct contravention of Saudi laws prohibiting the possession or use of opiates. Other incidents include the attempted use of plastic explosives against the Saudi infrastructure which would obviously endanger other Muslims making the *hajj*.

Despite such occasional problems, many Iranian Sunnis have come peacefully to Makkah and Madinah either to visit or to make the *hajj*. Some

Iranians have tried to reduce Shiʻa–Sunni tensions. Even Shah Muhammad Riza Pahlavi, although himself a Shiʻa, encouraged leading rich Iranian Sunnis to give job training and educational scholarships to Iranian Sunni students and also find them jobs.[33]

Islamic Solidarity

The Saudi–Iranian religious relationship has not always been negative, but has enjoyed a number of favourable aspects. The issue of Islamic solidarity, which was called for by King Faisal, is one of these positive aspects. Other issues like the creation of a number of Islamic institutions have also been considered as landmark efforts in the two countries' religious relationship.

The Issue of Islamic Solidarity
The Kingdom of Saudi Arabia was the first Islamic country to raise the issue of Islamic solidarity and express its deep concern about the future of the Islamic world. In 1955 the total population of the Islamic world was approximately 400 million. Differences and disputes between Islamic countries were numerous. Hence when King Saud ibn Abd al-Aziz paid a visit to Iran on 8 August 1955, he emphasized the need to solve the bilateral and multilateral disputes between the different Islamic countries. Shah Muhammad Riza Pahlavi expressed his full agreement with the King's proposition and promised to work in that direction. Almost ten years later, in 1964, King Faisal ibn Abd al-Aziz began his historic call to unite the Islamic world.

The summons was significant in that it came at a time when the Islamic nations were fragmented in their political, economic and religious goals, and when socialism and communism were finding footholds in many Arab and Muslim countries. King Faisal thus saw no alternative but to call for such unity among all Muslim nations. Acknowledging the fact that Iran was an important Islamic country, the King decided to pay a visit to Shah Muhammad Riza Pahlavi in 1965. Historically, the visit was very successful and the Shah agreed with King Faisal that the Islamic world needed such unity. In the mutual communiqué which was released at the end of the King's visit, the two monarchs agreed:

> It is necessary for the Islamic countries to study their problems, support their interests, develop their relationships and march unilaterally towards achieving the supra-Islamic goals for the prosperity of the Muslim nations, and to achieve social justice for them.[34]

The communiqué also emphasized an agreement between the two monarchs on the necessity of convening an Islamic Conference in which a chance would be given to discuss the mutual interests of the Islamic countries as a way of leading to unity and the maintenance of those interests. Islamic sentiments were reiterated during King Faisal's second visit to Iran in December 1967, when the two monarchs reaffirmed their commitment to the path of Islamic solidarity.

Although the Shah was in full agreement with King Faisal's call for Islamic solidarity, he was concerned that the call might be misinterpreted by the Western world and the wrong impression be given that Islam was against modernization. This view was actually an outcome of the Shah's opinion that religious classes were 'black reaction'.[35] He was thus keen that King Faisal should stress modern Islam and its strong elements supporting progress and modernity.

Further emphasis in this direction occurred when the Shah paid an official visit to Saudi Arabia in November 1968. In recognition of King Faisal's highly respected position in the Islamic world, the Shah, in his formal speech on 9 November, called the King 'Amir al-Muminin' (the Prince of Believers). Such recognition by the Shah, who represented a majority Shi'a state, was a major step towards uniting and solidifying the ranks of the Muslim *ummah*.

The Creation of Islamic Institutions
Another aspect of the two countries' religious co-operation may be seen in the creation of many Islamic organizations. The idea of creating and establishing such organizations was first addressed in 1926 during the first Islamic Conference. At that conference, the idea of creating an Islamic organization was only marginally discussed. The organization did not materialize since many of the Islamic countries were still under colonial rule and no direct challenge yet faced Islam as a religion.

With the emergence of a number of independent Islamic states in the 1940s and 1950s, the idea of creating an Islamic organization became more viable, and Saudi Arabia and Iran were both in favour. Thus, when the Pakistani Islamic Brotherhood Association called for an Islamic Conference to be held in Karachi in February 1949, both Saudi Arabia and Iran agreed to attend and also agreed to regard this association as an Islamic organization which would carry the name 'Organization of the Congress of the Islamic World'.[36] Two years later (9–12 January 1951), the organization held its second conference in Karachi and both Saudi Arabia and Iran attended. In fact, the 1951 conference confirmed the leading Islamic role of the

The Religious Relationship 1924–82

organization which by then had become more prominent in the Islamic world.[37]

The second major Islamic organization that these two countries helped create was the League of the Islamic World, set up in Makkah in May 1962. The establishment of this league was a milestone in the religious relationship between Saudi Arabia and the whole Islamic world, including Iran. Prior to the *hajj* season of 1962, King Faisal had sadly watched the unpleasant economic, political and social developments in the Islamic world carved out by the military ambitions of Arab and non-Arab Muslim leaders. Therefore, he called for an Islamic Conference to be held in Makkah immediately after the end of the Grand Pilgrimage of 1962. Fot its part, Iran agreed to attend the conference and Shah Muhammad Riza Pahlavi shared King Faisal's concerns.

To emphasize further the crucial importance of the conference, King Faisal (then Crown Prince of Saudi Arabia) chaired the working sessions, which began on 18 May 1962. After two days of discussions, the delegates decided, among other things, to establish a second Islamic organization to be called the Muslim World League. This organization was the brainchild of King Faisal and Iran was one of its founders. Makkah was chosen as the permanent headquarters. The founding assembly was also formed and consisted of 21 Islamic states, including Iran. The foundation of this highly regarded Islamic organization, which still functions very effectively throughout the Islamic world, was another milestone in the religious relationship between Saudi Arabia and Iran. Moreover, Iran is also a founding member of the various affiliated councils and agencies which belong to the Muslim World League.

A third major Islamic entity that both Saudi Arabia and Iran helped create is the Organization of the Islamic Conference (OIC), another brainchild of King Faisal. As early as 1969, the King envisaged the need for a regular annual conference between the leaders of the Islamic nations in order to discuss the public positions of Islam and its situation in the Islamic world. It was not until August of the same year that this idea became a necessity when a huge fire at al-Aqsa mosque in Jerusalem outraged the Islamic world and further encouraged the King to call for an Islamic Conference to be held in Rabat. The Shah responded favourably to the call and attended the conference himself. As an outcome of that conference, the OIC was created, and Jerusalem was chosen as its permanent headquarters. However, because Jerusalem was still under Israeli occupation, Jeddah was used as its temporary headquarters. Again, the establishment of this organization was another positive action on behalf of the religious relationship between Saudi Arabia and Iran.

Saudi–Iranian Relations 1932–1982

In later years, both countries showed great interest in co-operating and adopting similar Islamic positions, particularly during the meetings and conferences of the Foreign Ministers of Islamic countries, held under the auspices of the OIC. Such co-operation existed because Iran, under the Shah, considered itself a co-founder of the concept of unity among all Islamic countries. Shah Muhammad Riza Pahlavi was the first Muslim leader to raise the idea of creating an Islamic Common Market. Meanwhile, a state visit to Iran in 1968 by the Saudi acting Minister of Communications and *Hajj* paved the way for a much more organized Iranian pilgrimage. Beginning in 1970, the Iranian *hajj* missions were highly organized and included a medical team and a field hospital, which were to serve both Iranian and non-Iranian Muslims during the *hajj* season. Moreover, the Iranian pilgrims were among the richest and most generous pilgrims making the *hajj*. However, this situation changed dramatically after the 1979 revolution, with the coming of the ayatollahs' regime in Iran.

Religious Relations (1979–82)

Since 1979 the religious relationship between Saudi Arabia and Iran has deteriorated sharply. Throughout their bilateral religious history, the two countries have never experienced as much tension and rivalry as that which has divided them during this period. After the 1979 revolution, Iran was renamed the Islamic Republic of Iran. The name itself gave Iran a new dimension in its religious relationship with Saudi Arabia. This new dimension entailed considerable anti-Saudi positions throughout the Islamic world. The new Iranian regime has antagonized the Saudi government, encouraged the minority Shi'a to revolt against the Saudi state and used the *hajj* as a forum for exporting its Islamic revolution.

The Kingdom of Saudi Arabia, on the other hand, has exercised self-restraint and patience in dealing with these tactics in order to avoid confrontation with the new regime. In the meantime, the Saudi government has resorted to peaceful and meaningful talks with the Iranian authorities to avoid further deterioration in the religious as well as political relations between the two countries. However, Iran under the ayatollahs continues to put pressure on the Saudi government, particularly during the *hajj* season, demanding that the pilgrimage be politicized and sending enormous numbers of *hajjis* to the holy shrines each year.

With the outbreak of the Iran–Iraq war in 1980, and the Saudis' open support of Iraq, the religious and political relations between Saudi Arabia and Iran witnessed a further deterioration. Consequently, during the *hajj* seasons of 1980 and 1981, Iranian pilgrims were encouraged by their government to demonstrate in the streets of the holy places. The Saudi government approached the Iranian authorities to discuss these problems and in early 1982 the two governments began bilateral talks aimed at resolving these problems and guaranteeing a peaceful *hajj* season. Many of the talks were successful and the two sides were able to agree fully on many propositions. But the key issue was how to implement and execute what had been agreed upon.

In essence, there have been two Iranian factions struggling for power inside the country since the revolution: the radicals and the moderates. The first was strongly opposed to any kind of *rapprochement* with Saudi Arabia whereas, as one would expect, the second was in favour of achieving some kind of understanding with the Kingdom. Whenever the moderates agreed on some form of relationship with Saudi Arabia, the radicals would oppose it and sabotage the plan in an attempt to destroy the Saudi-Iranian religious understanding. Hence, the *hajj* season has been a great opportunity for the radicals to achieve this goal. The same approach has also been practised by the radicals in connection with other sensitive issues that have arisen between the two countries from time to time

The policy of antagonizing the Saudi government by Iran under Ayatollah Khomeini's regime was not limited to the *hajj* season. As early as 1980, the regime attempted to discredit Saudi Arabia and its leadership, and to question the capability of the Saudis to provide proper care for the two holy shrines. In other areas, they started to challenge Saudi authority over the two holy shrines (and continue to do so). An organized and expensive anti-Saudi propaganda campaign was carried out throughout the Arab and Islamic world. Daily newspapers were distributed free of charge, hundreds of books and booklets were published, video tapes and cassettes were produced and distributed in the Western world, and pamphlets and leaflets were distributed inside the mosques, particularly on Fridays—all in an attempt to discredit Saudi Arabia.

However, the feather which broke the camel's back, as the Arabs say, was the Iranian claim that the Kingdom of Saudi Arabia was not capable of managing the two holy shrines' affairs, and that a joint Islamic committee was needed to look after Makkah and Madinah. At this juncture, Saudi patience ran out. The kingdom waged a counter-campaign spelling out the misdeeds of the Iranian regime and labelling it as 'non-Islamic'. Subsequently, religious relations have declined daily and are still declining.

An additional facet of the Iranian anti-Saudi campaign was terrorism. Beginning in 1981, Iran resorted to terrorism in order to destabilize the Kingdom. Iran carried out a number of minor terrorist actions inside Saudi

Arabia and against some Saudi diplomats. It took advantage of the Lebanese civil war, using some of the Lebanese Shi'a groups to carry out its terrorist activities against Saudi Arabia and to train its own terrorist squads in Lebanon. Many terrorist training camps were also opened inside Iran for this and other purposes.

Believing in the Islamic principles of peace and justice, the Kingdom of Saudi Arabia has never intended to harm Iran or return hatred with hatred. Instead, its approach has been based on logic, peaceful negotiations and meaningful talks. Moreover, the Kingdom strongly believes that Iran could play a very positive role in uniting and solidifying the ranks of the Islamic nations. It is true that Iran has the potential for becoming an active member of Islamic society. Co-operating with Saudi Arabia and other Islamic countries is necessary for Iran in order to restore its lost credibility in the Islamic world. Eager to see Iran abandon its anti-Saudi activities, the Kingdom of Saudi Arabia will not spare any effort that would bring Iran back into the fold of the Islamic world. However, Iran under the ayatollahs has to desire such a role.

Conclusion

Both Saudi Arabia and Iran are Muslim nations. Their Islamic history and their contribution to Islamic culture oblige them to co-operate and co-ordinate their efforts in serving Islam at its best. The religious relationship that existed between the two countries during the time of the Pahlavi dynasty proved to be in the interests of both countries as well as in the interests of the Islamic world as a whole. Their close religious ties during the 1960s and 1970s resulted in the creation and establishment of a number of internationally recognized Islamic organizations which are playing positive roles in uniting the Islamic nations and solving their problems.

On the other hand, the religious confrontation between Saudi Arabia and Iran under the ayatollahs is not in anyone's interests or even in the interests of the Islamic *ummah*. Sectarian and ideological differences should be overlooked, particularly by present-day Iran. And the focus should be on adhering to the basic principles of Islam. If Iran abandoned its anti-Saudi rhetoric, both countries would unquestionably achieve great success in the area of Islamic solidarity. From the Saudi point of view, such a goal is possible and achievable, and the ball is in the Iranian court.

5
Economic Relations 1932–82

Historical Overview

Saudi–Iranian economic relations are based almost entirely on oil; the two countries have relatively few other commercial ties. For example, according to the *Iran Almanac* of 1974 and 1975, Iran's imports from Saudi Arabia and Iran's non-oil exports to the Kingdom from 1969 to 1974 were as shown in Tables 4 and 5.

Table 4. Iran's Imports from Saudi Arabia, 1969–74 ('000 Iranian riyals; US$1 = IR60)

1969/70	1970/71	1971/72	1972/73	1973/74
524	37.356	50.058	42.587	7.729

Table 5. Iran's Non-oil Exports to Saudi Arabia, 1969–74 ('000 Iranian riyals; US$1 = IR60)

1969/70	1970/71	1971/72	1972/73	1973/74
75.235	118.235	289.495	340.341	560.927

Modern economic relations, however, were not originally based on oil. Saudi Arabia did not really become a modern oil state until after the Second World War, and although oil was discovered in Iran (or Persia as it was known then) in 1908, it did not come to dominate the Iranian economy for many years.

Prior to oil relations, the greatest volume of direct trade between Saudi Arabia and Iran came as a result of the annual *hajj*, when thousands of Iranians trekked across Arabia to the holy cities and back, a trip that could take months. The Iranian *hajjis* bought items of subsistence from local merchants, often selling carpets to raise the money. To this day, small carpets are still used as a type of rudimentary traveller's cheque by Iranians, Afghans and Pakistanis making the pilgrimage.

Saudi–Iranian economic relations can be divided into three distinct periods: the early years (1924–41), when modern economic relations were in their infancy; the developmental years (1941–60), when their growing wealth and economic interests greatly accelerated economic relations; and the contemporary period (1969–82). Before looking at those periods, however, it will be helpful to review briefly the modern economic development of each state.

Saudi Arabia: A Brief Economic Overview

Except for oil, Saudi Arabia has few natural resources. Its broad land mass (2,250,000 sq. km) is mostly desert and could historically support few people. The country can be divided into three economic areas: western Saudi Arabia, made up of the Hijaz and Asir; central Saudi Arabia, or Najd; and eastern Saudi Arabia, called the Eastern Province and comprised of al-Hasa and al-Qatif oases and various towns and cities along the Gulf coast.

Prior to the discovery of oil, only the Hijaz had a fairly well-developed cash economy, based almost entirely on receipts from the annual *hajj*. There was also some subsistence agriculture in the Hijaz mountains and fishing in the Red Sea. Najd and the Eastern Province had subsistence economies. The former consisted of nomadic pastoralism and subsistence agriculture in scattered oasis townships. Dates were grown as a principal cash crop. Al-Hasa and al-Qatif also engaged in subsistence agriculture, including date production, and on the coast, fishing and pearl diving were the principal occupations.

When King Abd al-Aziz ibn Abd al-Rahman Al Saud, then Sultan of Najd, captured the Hijaz in 1924–25, receipts from the *hajj* became the principal source of government revenue. The three to four month *hajj* season (now reduced to four to six weeks due to modern means of transportation) accounted for most of the commercial retail trade of the country, mainly resale of imports to *hajjis*.[1] King Abd al-Aziz had also received subsidies from the British, but they were cut off in 1924.[2]

Under King Abd al-Aziz, economic policies for the newly united country were based on Islamic law, which emphasized a market economy and private enterprise. Due to a chronic shortage of funds, economic development plans in the early years were rudimentary at best. Nevertheless, the King persevered in his efforts to look after the economic welfare of his subjects. His first step in that direction was to create a socio-economic programme under the name of *al-hijar*, which means 'agricultural settlements'.[3] This programme was aimed at settling the nomads, particularly those who had served in the King's bedouin military forces, in areas close to the very few available sources of water, underground wells. The government provided the settlers with the necessary agricultural equipment and seed to cultivate their lands, and sent tutors to teach the settlers and their children how to read and write and to instruct them in the fundamentals of Islam. On balance, the programme was a very successful socio-economic endeavour and was later expanded. The government undertook other economic and social development programmes during this period, including the search for water and the building of roads. However, due to a shortage of funds, the programmes were very modest, particularly compared to those of the 1960s and 1970s.

In the years before oil, retail commerce and the *hajj* service industry dominated the private sector. One of King Abd al-Aziz's earliest priorities was to create commercial regulations to guide the private sector and prevent abuses. Moreover, he created commercial incentives such as low taxes and low trade levies. The Hanbali school of Islamic jurisprudence, which underpins the Saudi constitutional system, is one of the most pro-business schools of Islamic law, and it was no accident that the King sought to strengthen private enterprise. In 1932 he created the Ministry of Finance, to implement commercial as well as economic and fiscal policies. With oil revenues, the Saudi private sector greatly expanded, and in 1954 a separate Ministry of Commerce was created.

Saudi Arabia entered the oil age in 1938, when its first producing well, Dammam No. 7, began producing in commercial quantities, but it was not until after the Second World War that the Kingdom began to accrue oil wealth in appreciable quantities, and the 1960s before it was in a position to begin systematic economic planning.

The 1930s witnessed a severe worldwide economic recession from which the Kingdom of Saudi Arabia was not immune. Due to economic hardship, fewer Muslims made the *hajj*, drastically reducing *hajj* receipts, and consequently, government revenues. This had a great effect on the overall economy of the country. The world depression was not the only factor adversely affecting the Saudi economy, however. Throughout the 1930s the clouds of war began to gather, not only in Europe, but throughout the Muslim world. By late in the decade, many Muslim communities were barred from making the *hajj* for geopolitical reasons as well as economic ones. In Saudi Arabia's darkest hour economically, events were transpiring that were ultimately to transform the Saudi economy beyond anyone's wildest dreams—the discovery of oil.[4]

Oil exploration had gone on intermittently for years in what is now the Kingdom before it was discovered. The British had looked for oil in the Hijaz in 1922. The following year a New Zealand investor, Major Frank Holmes, obtained a concession to explore for oil in Najd. At the time, Sultan Abd al-Aziz did not really want his country opened up to the foreign political exploitation he believed would follow the discovery of oil, nor did he believe there was any oil there in the first place, but he needed the money a concession would bring. The concession lapsed in 1928, but in 1933 Socal (Standard Oil of California) obtained another concession from Abd al-Aziz, now King of Saudi Arabia. The King was by now actively seeking a concession to augment his dwindling revenues.

Drilling began near the Gulf coast in 1935 with Dammam No. 1 well. Dammam No. 7 was spudded in 1936, and in 1938 began producing over 1,500 barrels a day. Saudi Arabia had entered the oil age. Socal created a producing company, California Arabian Standard Oil Company (CASOC). In 1936 Texaco bought a half interest in CASOC and in 1944 CASOC's name was changed to the Arabian American Oil Company, ARAMCO. In 1948 Mobil and Esso (EXXON) also bought equity in ARAMCO.[5]

In 1973 the Saudi government acquired a 25 per cent interest in ARAMCO. That interest increased to 60 per cent in the next year. In 1980, with retroactive financial effect to 1976, the participation interest increased to 100 per cent when Saudi Arabia purchased all of ARAMCO's remaining equity. Today the company is known as Saudi ARAMCO and is the largest oil company in the Kingdom.[6]

The discovery of oil did not have an immediate economic effect on the country. The world slump in the 1930s kept prices depressed and increasing conflict leading up to the Second World War disrupted markets. For a time, the Saudi treasury was kept solvent by advances from Socal and Texaco. In 1943 the United States made Saudi Arabia eligible for Lend-Lease aid in an effort to keep the Kingdom financially afloat. It was not until after the war, therefore, that the Kingdom began to accrue oil revenues of any magnitude. And it was many years after that before Saudi Arabia had sufficient economic and social infrastructure to absorb large investments in development projects.

Economic Relations 1932–82

Economic infrastructure developed over a long period of time. The first Western bank was the Netherlands Trading Society, the 'Dutch Bank', which had been established in Jeddah in the Western Province in the 1920s to service the banking needs of *hajjis* from the Dutch East Indies (now Indonesia). In the 1940s other foreign banks were allowed to operate in the Kingdom and branches of British, French and American banks were established. In 1951 the Kingdom established a central bank, the Saudi Arabian Monetary Agency (SAMA), to stabilize the currency, regularize government financial transactions, regulate the private banks and manage the Kingdom's reserves.[7]

Public resistance to modern banking practices had still to be overcome, however, and all banking practices had to be made to conform to Islamic law. Many citizens preferred the traditional foreign exchange dealers such as al-Ka'ki and Salim ibn Mahfuz. These two actually began their own bank, the Saudi Arabian Bank, in 1952.[8]

The Saudis traditionally preferred transacting business with gold and silver coins, distrusting paper notes. In 1953 SAMA issued scrip called '*hajj receipts*' in exchange for foreign currencies which could be exchanged for goods and services and redeemed at any bank. The local merchants, who would have resisted paper notes, accepted the scrip which then began to circulate locally—an ingenious way to introduce paper money.[9]

By the reign of King Faisal ibn Abd al-Aziz (1964–75), the Kingdom was ready for more rapid economic development, and the King became a champion of the modernization of the country. 'Like it or not,' he once said, 'we must join the modern world and find an honourable place in it.'[10] King Faisal set the development philosophy for the Kingdom which remains to this day: the attainment of technical modernization while rejecting the secularization of most of the Western world. Saudi social objectives and moral and cultural values have always been tied closely to the principles of Islam. For example, among the development projects to which the King paid considerable attention was the expansion and restoration of the two holy mosques in Makkah and Madinah as well as many other holy shrines.

Since 1970 the Kingdom has had four five-year development plans. The first plan (1970–75) focused on the social and administrative infrastructure. It introduced new programmes emphasizing the development of the nation's human resources through extensive investment in education and training. The second plan (1975–80) focused on physical infrastructure, such as roads, ports, airports and desalination plants to augment water supplies. The third plan (1980–85) focused upon consolidating the gains made in the first two plans. It also emphasized 'economic diversification', which is one of the predominant objectives of the entire development process, despite Saudi

Arabia's overwhelming dependence on the oil sector. The fourth plan (1985-90) concentrated on further human and economic resource development.

With an essentially oil-based economy, Saudi industrial diversification is based mainly on petrochemicals, or on the use of oil and gas to power industrial processes. Petrochemical plants, such as plastics and fertilizers, are concentrated in two huge industrial complexes, one at Yanbu' on the Red Sea and the other at Jubail, on the Gulf. They are among the largest and most modern industrial complexes in the world today. In addition to the heavy investment in government-owned plants, the Kingdom has continued to make a concerted effort to develop and expand the private sector, using incentives such as long-term, interest-free loans. Currently, there are approximately 2,991 industrial projects in Saudi Arabia.

Saudi development policies have always attempted to move the country forward at a measured pace so that the society could adjust to the changes taking place. By the 1970s, however, it was on the threshold of a major expansion. Economic development programmes were greatly expanded as a result of the major increase in oil revenues that began with the energy crisis of 1973 and lasted to the end of the decade. The pace of development continued at a dizzying pace throughout the 1970s, threatening the society's ability to keep up. In the 1980s, with the oil glut and declining revenues, the Kingdom took a more measured look at development, and adopted policies designed to consolidate its impressive gains.

Despite the rapid accelerated pace of development in the 1970s, however, the planners avoided the over-investment, inflation and social as well as economic dislocations that accompanied economic development in Iran and contributed to the overthrow of the monarchy.

Iran: A Brief Economic Overview
In 1923-24, when Riza Khan first came to power, Persia was a large, populous country (12 million people) with relatively abundant resources compared to its Arab neighbours. The economy was based primarily on agriculture, and state revenues came mainly from customs, internal taxes and state lands. Although a British oil concessionaire, William Knox D'Arcy, had found oil in 1908, the government received only 16 per cent of the net oil revenues from the British-owned Anglo-Persian (later Anglo-Iranian) Oil Company. The British not only found the oil, but were the major financial beneficiaries as well.[11]

Riza Khan (later Riza Pahlavi) quickly consolidated his power, deposing the Qajar dynasty and assuming the title of Shah in 1925. Greatly influenced by the reforms of Kemal Ataturk of Turkey, he set out to transform Iran into a strong, modern, secular state. A major target was the powerful Shi'a clergy, which he believed constituted a major threat to the regime and to the modernization process.

Most of Riza Shah's reforms were social (e.g. ordering the use of Western dress and abolishing the veiling of women), administrative (e.g. overhauling government operations and creating a modern bureaucracy) or political (e.g. consolidating power in his own hands and creating a modern army). Economically, he instituted infrastructure projects—transportation, communication facilities and power plants, as well as building state-owned industries—and created a new bureaucracy to run them. He also attempted to break the power of the traditional merchant class ('the bazaar'), which resisted economic modernization.

It was not until after the Second World War, under Riza Shah's son, Muhammad Riza Shah, that the oil sector came to dominate the Iranian economy. In 1951 Prime Minister Mossadeq nationalized Iranian oil with disastrous results for the economy. In 1954, however, an agreement was reached with a consortium of Western oil companies recognizing the nationalization and stipulating a fifty-fifty split in revenues.[12] These Western companies no longer owned the concession, however; the oil was technically owned by the newly created National Iranian Oil Company (NIOC). In 1973 NIOC took over complete control of oil production and the era of foreign dependence was over.[13]

The period from 1954 to the Islamic revolution in 1979 was one of high investment in economic development projects. Unlike Saudi Arabia's more deliberate pace of development, this investment was often uneven and ill-considered, often exceeding what Iran's limited financial and human resources could absorb. Agricultural reform was a high priority. Iran is a fertile land by Middle Eastern standards, with arable land and adequate natural rainfall, particularly in the northern part of the country. Most of the land, however, was owned by a few families in what was basically a feudal system. In 1963 the Shah announced a broad reform programme called the White Revolution which called for land redistribution and the abolition of the absentee landlord–peasant system of agriculture, as well as social and political reforms such as granting suffrage to women and initiating a major literacy campaign. Over time, the White Revolution was expanded and efforts were made to diversify and expand the economy. Programmes were developed to expand social and economic infrastructure, develop mineral resources such as iron, lead, zinc, copper and uranium, create an industrial sector, overhaul the banking industry and make the government bureaucracy more efficient and responsive to public need.[14]

When the price of oil quadrupled to almost $12 per barrel in 1973, the resulting oil boom boosted government revenues to unprecedented levels. Oil revenues accounted for roughly 95 per cent of foreign exchange earnings.[15] Ironically, the boom heralded the downfall of the monarchy. With huge financial resources at his disposal, the Shah became intent on converting Iran into a mighty industrial power within 20 years. Investment in all sectors of the economy occurred at such a rapid pace that it outstripped the ability of the economy to absorb it, creating massive inflation. Huge amounts were also spent in building up Iran's military forces, another inflationary step.

For example, whereas Iran had been a net exporter of food before the White Revolution, the agricultural sector almost collapsed in the 1970s. Peasants were given even less help by government agricultural agents than by their previous landlords (who were motivated by profit) and productivity declined. The situation was exacerbated as thousands of peasants moved to the cities to take higher-paying construction and other jobs created by the Shah's accelerated development projects. Faced with both food shortages and inflation, the government had to import food but also subsidized prices rather than the farmers, driving agricultural profits down even further. The industrial sector fared little better: workers demanded higher wages because of inflation, but their wages were not matched by higher productivity, creating yet more inflation.

The whole process was kept afloat by oil revenues, but in 1976 oil prices declined and the government was forced to take politically disastrous austerity measures. In short, the White Revolution had become a 'white elephant'. The economic dislocation resulting from over-investment during the 1970s was a major cause of the downfall of the Shah's regime. One of the main reasons behind the disastrous results of the Shah's development programme was that, unlike Saudi Arabia, he attempted to do too much too fast. The country was neither economically nor socially ready to absorb such massive development investment so quickly.

After the Shah's downfall in 1979 at the hands of the Shi'a clergy, the Iranian economy faced a real dilemma. The new leaders faced an economy that was a shambles. Labour strikes, peasant uprisings and turmoil among the bazaar merchants spread throughout Iran. Many economic programmes and development projects had been halted and others suffered great losses. Matters were made even worse as technocrats fled the country and the clergy enacted stringent laws and restrictions on economic development as counter to their idea of Islam.

The situation intensified in September 1980 as a result of the outbreak of the Iraq–Iran war, which had a negative impact on every sector of the economy. Although oil exports were maintained, domestic oil supplies were disrupted and many factories and industries were closed down. Other projects had to be revised and some were cancelled. Moreover, all development plans were squeezed and in some years were entirely put on hold. In short, the eight-year war (1980–88) devastated Iran's economy. The regime coped only by placing incredible suffering on the people. One of the very few pluses of this period was that Iran emerged from the war with little foreign debt.

The magnitude of the consequences of the Iran–Iraq war on the Iranian economy by 1990 can be seen in a few statistics. During the war, the annual inflation rate reached 40 per cent, the unemployment rate reached 25 per cent of the workforce and the *per capita* income declined from $2,400 in 1977 to $1,300 in 1987.[16]

Just as economic chaos was instrumental in the overthrow of the Shah's regime, it was also instrumental in Iran's decision to disengage from the Iran–Iraq war in 1988. Opposition to disengagement was strong, but former Majlis Speaker Hashemi Rafsanjani succeeded in making economic reconstruction the top priority. The task before Rafsanjani is formidable, but Iran is making steady progress. By the end of the 1990s, unless there is another destructive domestic or external crisis, Iran should be well along the way to recovery.

Economic Relations

A central consideration of both Saudi Arabia and Iran in all their bilateral relations—political, religious, economic and military—is the insistence on respect for their independence and prestige. Mutual consideration and self-esteem have always been of great significance to both countries, and while both have been willing to expand bilateral relations in many different fields, neither has been willing to do so at the cost of its prestige and independence. Thus Saudi–Iranian bilateral economic relations developed in a very cautious and calculated manner, beginning with limited trade and commercial ventures.

The Early Years (1924–41)
Before 1932 economic relations between Persia and the Arabian peninsula were restricted mainly to commercial dealings surrounding the *hajj*. It was a one-sided relationship between Hijazi, Najdi and al-Hasa merchants and Persian *hajjis*, limited to a specific season and not organized. Persian pilgrims visiting the Hijaz region to visit the holy cities and perform their annual pilgrimage brought commercial goods to sell in the Hijaz markets.

Persian goods like rice, spices, sugar, tea, dried fish products, cotton, textiles and handmade Persian rugs were always in demand in the Hijazi markets and other markets of the Arabian peninsula. Through a number of Arab Gulf sheikhdoms such as Bahrain, Oman and Dubai, Persian goods were re-exported to the markets of the Eastern Province of the Kingdom. But again, the volume of this trade was limited and not well organized.

Two broader issues with economic implications involving Saudi Arabia and Persia transpired during these years, one concerning the expansion of air routes in the region and the other slavery. In 1928 both the Kingdom and Persia faced a common issue with the British government related to the air routes which dominated the Gulf region. Britain wanted to establish two air routes along the shores of the Gulf to service its commercial and military interests in the region. The first was on the southern Persian shore of the Gulf, and the second extended along the Arabian littoral with a refuelling stop in the Hasa region.[17] The initial response to the British proposal from both the Saudi and Persian governments was negative.

King Abd al-Aziz's reply illustrated his great reluctance to open up the Kingdom to outside influences, even for economic gain and despite the fact that he greatly needed the revenues. Having observed other countries, he was convinced that economic penetration would not only be socially disruptive, but would be followed by attempts at political penetration as well. The King replied to the British that he could not agree to the air route because of the attitude of the Hasa tribes, whose suspicions had been aroused by the establishment of military posts in the southern desert of Iraq.

Riza Shah's objections reflected his own political ambitions as well as economic considerations. He objected to the air route because it did not cross central Persia and he wanted a Baghdad–Hamadan–Tehran–Karachi route.[18] The Shah, however, also wanted complete tariff autonomy for his country (the tariffs were then under British control). He agreed to permit the British-owned Imperial Airways to run a service along the south Persian coast for a period of three years in return for Britain's relinquishing autonomy over Iranian tariffs.

The second issue that arose during this period concerned the slave trade. House slavery had been practised in the region from ancient times and bore virtually no relation to the brutal institution that developed in the Western hemisphere in the eighteenth and nineteenth centuries. In the tribally based societies of the region, personal status was conferred, not individually, but by association with a kinship group. Some families were from ruling tribes; others were very lowly. The status of slaves was derived from the status of their owners, and lowly as that might have been, it was still better than a tribeless person who had no status at all.

Some slave families amassed considerable wealth and power. Indeed, a former Saudi Minister of Finance came from a slave family and at one time was one of the richest men in the world. Nevertheless, the institution was rapidly becoming an anachronism in the region as it moved toward modernity, and the British, who were the dominant outside power, sought to wipe it out completely.

Slave trading was one of the most active and lucrative commercial activities among the Gulf states, including Persia. By the 1920s it emanated mainly from Persian Baluchistan, where slaves were sent to Oman and the Trucial Coast. From the Trucial Coast, many were transported to the interior, including Najd. British efforts were aimed mainly at Persia's involvement in slave trading, rather than at slave-holding in the Arabian peninsula. Persia was a signatory to two anti-slavery conventions: in 1882 the Persian government signed a convention with Britain, banning Persia from further slave trade; and in 1926 the Persian government signed the slavery convention of the League of Nations.[19]

Quite apart from considerations of profit, Persia objected to the 1882 convention on the grounds that it encroached on Persian sovereignty and was therefore derogatory to Persian dignity.[20] The convention gave Britain the right to search Persian vessels on the high seas, both in the Gulf and in Persian territorial waters.

Faced with a unilateral abrogation of the convention, Britain appeared willing to give in on the issue of searching Persian vessels in return for a reaffirmation of banning slavery. The British Residency in India recommended that:

> If there were a unilateral denunciation of the 1882 Convention, Persia as a member of the League of Nations should be pressed to take steps as soon as it is clear that it had failed to suppress the slave traffic. The right of searching vessels in Persian territorial waters at present exercised by His Majesty's Government under the Slavery Convention might be abandoned should some further concession be necessary.[21]

Nevertheless, British–Persian talks on slavery broke down and the Persians continued to engage in the slave traffic between Iran and the Arab Gulf coast for some time. By 1970, however, slavery was officially banned throughout the region, although many former slaves refused to leave their masters.[22]

In 1929 Riza Shah and King Abd al-Aziz signed a Treaty of Friendship between Persia and the Kingdom of the Hijaz, Najd and its Dependencies. Considered a turning-point in the two countries' bilateral relations, the treaty focused primarily on the establishment of diplomatic relations, but dealt with other aspects of overall relations as well. Article 4 stated: 'The two honourable parties announce their desire for exchanging other supplementary memorandums, in due time, in order to sign agreements dealing with political, commercial, economic, and other affairs...'[23] Thus, while the treaty did not spell out any specific commercial or economic terms, it did set the stage for the development of bilateral, including economic, relations. This beginning could be said to have come to fruition on 1 January 1972, when the two countries signed their first economic co-operation agreement in Jeddah.[24]

During the 1930s bilateral trade relations continued to expand, albeit sporadically. A new element was the appearance of commercial agents in the Kingdom. These were Saudi merchants of Iranian origin, who had immigrated to Hijaz and other regions of the Kingdom, and who acted as commercial representatives and agents for Iranian merchants wishing to trade with the Arabian peninsula.[25] Through their efforts, bilateral trade relations became much more organized, though the volume of trade continued to fluctuate according to economic conditions. In 1961 Bank Melli Iran established a branch in the Kingdom, another step towards the establishment of stronger economic ties between the two countries. Ten years later, however, the bank merged with al-Jazirah Bank.

The Great Depression of the 1930s, followed by the gradual expansion of hostilities leading to the Second World War, greatly retarded commercial relations between the two countries. As the number of Iranian *hajjis* decreased, trade fell to its lowest level in modern times. When in 1941 Riza Shah abdicated in favour of his son Muhammad Riza Shah and Allied forces occupied Iran, bilateral trade virtually ceased.

The Developmental Years (1941–60)
The construction of bilateral trade relations, which had begun in the 1930s with the world depression and the expanding military conflict that led to the Second World War, continued in the early 1940s due to the war itself. The Saudi economy began the decade in desperate straits. Although oil had been found in commercial quantities, the Kingdom had to wait for the end of the war before economically significant oil production could begin. In the meantime, with *hajj* receipts virtually halted due to the war, the Kingdom was forced to subsist on advances from future royalties from the oil companies. In 1943 the US government stepped in with a Lend–Lease agreement, largely to keep the Saudi treasury afloat.

All that changed radically after the war as Saudi oil came on stream. In January 1945 ARAMCO also began construction of the Trans-Arabian pipeline (TAPLINE), running between the oilfields in the Eastern Province and the port of Sidon in Lebanon.[26] Completed in 1950, TAPLINE further enhanced Saudi oil shipments by providing an outlet on the Mediterranean. Within a very few years, the Kingdom was transformed from one of the poorest countries in the world into a major oil power.

In some respects, Iran, while its economy was far better off than the Saudi economy during and immediately after the war, fared even worse than the Kingdom during this period. Iran was under foreign occupation during the war and in 1941 Riza Shah was forced to abdicate by the British. Following the war, a further political crisis was created when the Soviets sought to carve out enclaves in northern Iran. Finally, in the early 1950s a wave of xenophobic nationalism swept over Iran under Prime Minister Mossadeq. His nationalization of Iranian oilfields in 1951 without compensation halted Iranian production for a time and created huge strains on the economy.

Nevertheless, with rapidly expanding oil revenues in the 1950s, both countries experienced considerable economic prosperity, and trade relations again expanded. Both countries pursued *laissez faire* commercial policies and, for the most part, this trade was carried on in the private sector with very little government regulation. One exception was the *hajj* trade, at least to the degree that the Saudi government continued to make every effort to ensure that foreign *hajjis* were treated fairly during this holy pilgrimage.

Another exception involved the Arab economic boycott of Israel. The history of Arabs boycotting zionist and Jewish businesses goes back to 1922 when there was initial and, as it turned out, prophetic concern that Jewish immigration into Palestine would undermine the overwhelmingly Arab character of the country.[27] Until 1950 these boycott activities had been directed at commerce between the Arab states and zionists living in the part of Palestine that the Jews had seized control of as Israel.

In 1951 the Arab League created a Central Boycott Office, located in Damascus. Its function was to monitor foreign trade with Israel and encourage Arab states to prevent this trade, which was considered 'smuggling'. In September 1952 the Arab League recommended the Arab boycott of all third-country companies with branches in Israel, and in April 1953 the League decided to take its first formal boycott action.[28] The League's decision bound all Arab states to boycott companies, regardless of their nationality or where they were located, that had trade and commercial ties with Israel. Since Iran did not implement the Arab boycott and because it had close trade relations with Israel dating back to the creation of the zionist state in 1948—Israel was a major purchaser of Iranian oil—Iranian trade relations with Saudi Arabia were bound to suffer. In 1958, the first year for which there are available trade figures, there was a marginal balance of trade, with no substantial change over the following three years. Figures 2[29] and 3[30] show the value of Iranian–Israeli and Israeli–Iranian exports in 1958 and 1966.

Figure 2. Iran–Israel Economic Exchange, 1958 (million US$)

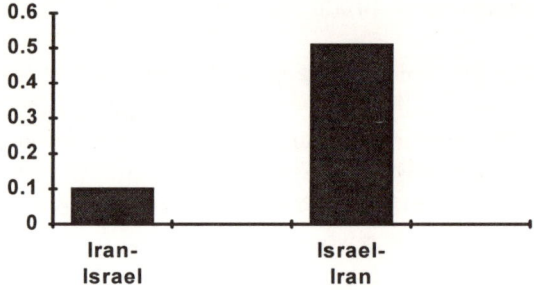

Figure 3. Iran–Israel Economic Exchange, 1966 (million US$)

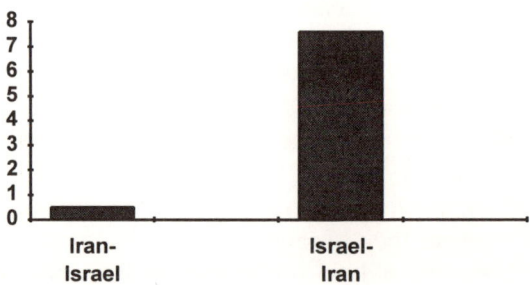

Economic Relations 1932–82

Iran's commercial ties with Israel during this period did not necessarily hinder private trade between Saudi Arabia and Iran, but they did hamper official government-to-government economic relations for some years. For example, when the Shah visited Saudi Arabia in 1957, the official communiqué issued at the end of the visit did not mention the economic or trade relations between the two countries.[31]

The Contemporary Period (1960–82)
With the beginning of the 1960s, official Saudi–Iranian economic relations took a new turn. The emergence of Saudi Arabia and Iran as two of the leading oil producers in OPEC resulted in greatly expanded economic relations. Between 1964 and 1966 the volume of Iranian trade with the Gulf states, including Saudi Arabia, tripled. Iranian exports to the Kingdom in 1964 are estimated at IR 10,057 million (IR = US$60).[32] Commercial relations were given a further boost in the aftermath of the 1967 Arab–Israeli war with the Shah's condemnation of the Israeli occupation of Arab land and his call for an immediate withdrawal. Close Iranian political as well as commercial ties with Israel had long been an impediment to closer Saudi–Iranian relations, and the Shah's position on the occupied territories greatly cleared the air. On 29 June 1967 the two countries signed a civil air memorandum which regularized the ground–air services to be provided by each country to the other country's airline. That was followed by an agreement signed between Saudi Arabian Airlines and Iran Air allowing all Iranian pilgrims to fly Iran Air on their way to perform the *hajj*.[33]

In this improved atmosphere, official visits to both countries increased as officials explored new channels for economic co-operation. In July 1968 the President of the Board of Directors of NIOC paid a visit to the Kingdom, where he had constructive talks with the Saudi Oil Minister and other Saudi officials. The following month, the Saudi Oil Minister returned the visit, accompanied by Prince Sa'ad al-Faisal, son of the late King Faisal and a member of the Saudi Ministry of Petroleum and Minerals at the time.

During the Shah's subsequent state visit to Saudi Arabia from 9 to 14 November 1968, he raised the subject of establishing an Islamic Common Market. And the visit opened the door for a broader range of economic and trade ties between the two states. On 27 April 1970 Iran's Minister of the Economy headed a delegation to Saudi Arabia to explore means for the further expansion of economic and commercial relations between his country and the Kingdom. The visit was returned by the Saudi Minister of Commerce and Industries on 25 May 1970. During that return visit, an agreement was reached between the two countries that stated they should co-operate in shipping ventures in the Gulf region, and that Iranian merchants should visit Saudi Arabia in order to promote business with their Saudi counterparts.[34] This was followed by an exhibition of Iranian goods suitable for Saudi markets, which took place in Tehran on 25 July 1970 and was visited by a number of Saudi merchants and businessmen.[35] In December 1970, in accordance with the May agreement, an Iranian economic delegation visited the Kingdom with the aim of removing all barriers to the expansion of commercial relations; it was also agreed that Iran would hold an industrial exhibition in Saudi Arabia.

The growth in bilateral commercial ties reached a high point on 1 January 1972 with the signing of a formal commercial treaty during a visit to Saudi Arabia by the Under-Secretary of the Iranian Ministry of Economic Affairs. Both parties also announced that they would make joint investments in industrial projects in the other's country.[36]

Iranian efforts to foster closer commercial ties stemmed from more than improved political relations, however. Iran was trying to establish itself as a trading and manufacturing centre in the markets in the Gulf and India, East Africa, and both Eastern and Western Europe.[37] Thus the Shah and his ministers were busy conducting high-level economic talks, not only with the Saudis, but with British, Japanese and Chinese officials. The Shah even sent the NIOC Chairman to South Africa to open what was called an NIOC refinery.[38]

Of far more importance than expanded bilateral commercial relations was the expansion of relations dealing with the commodity that made expanded trade relations possible: oil. The years between 1960 and 1973 were momentous for the oil-exporting countries. At the beginning of the period, they had virtually no control over what was without exception their most important natural resource. Production and price-setting were controlled by international oil companies that had obtained concessions from host governments to explore for and exploit all oil and gas found in the concession areas as they saw fit. Iran had cancelled the concessions and nationalized its oil resources in 1951, but following a settlement with the former concessionaires, its oil industry was still controlled by an international consortium of oil companies and Iran had no real control despite its ownership.

In order to gain more control over their oil resources, the major oil-exporting countries, led by Venezuela, created the Organization of Petroleum Exporting Countries in September 1960. Because of the buyers' market that existed throughout the 1960s, OPEC initially had very little influence. By 1970, however, the picture had begun to change. Demand had been growing faster than supply for some years, and when in 1970 the United States became a net importer, oil became a sellers' market. With an international shortage of oil, the exporting countries were able to wrest control of their oil resources from the companies in 1971.

For Iran, which already owned its oil, the task of actually running its own oil production operations entailed having the state oil company, NIOC, take over from the consortium. For Saudi Arabia, as well as Qatar and the UAE which followed its lead, the process was different. They gradually bought out the equity of the foreign-owned producing companies, ARAMCO in the case of Saudi Arabia.

The acquisition process was called 'participation', and was first introduced in a speech at the American University of Beirut in 1967 by the Saudi Oil Minister, Sheikh Ahmad Zaki Yamani. Yamani explained that by providing for phased buy-out over several years, participation was superior to nationalization because it kept the companies in the game. Otherwise, he feared, once the companies lost their equity, they would have little incentive to maintain stable prices and everyone would suffer.[39] Thus Saudi Arabia negotiated a participation agreement whereby it bought a 25 per cent interest in ARAMCO in 1973, increased its equity share to 60 per cent in 1974 and purchased the remaining equity in 1980. Saudi Arabia, along with other members of OPEC, won effective control of its oil resources in 1971 in agreements with the oil companies that ended the latter's monopolistic powers in setting price and production rates.

Saudi and Iranian interests coincided in their mutual desire to gain control of their own oil industries from the companies, but within OPEC their interests often diverged. Both countries vied for leadership of the organization and differed on what OPEC policies should be. Saudi Arabia was the leader of those countries that wanted moderate price rises and stable prices. Iran was one of the price hawks that wanted to boost the price as high as it would go.

For the Shah, leadership of OPEC was in great part a reflection of his imperial ambitions. Moreover, Iran had been the world's leading oil-exporting country until it nationalized its oil in 1951. Although it never again became the dominant supplier, it continued as a leading exporter and the Shah's aspirations dominated OPEC policy as the swing producer. In the meantime, Saudi Arabia, which had only minimal production at the end of the Second World War, had risen to be the leading exporter. With smaller domestic oil needs and far more reserves than Iran, it had more productive capacity and could afford to export a greater percentage of its production. Thus Saudi Arabia and not Iran became the swing producer in OPEC in the 1970s.

The rivalry over price and production policies was also driven by some very real economic factors. The Shah believed that Iran, with a large population and many natural resources other than oil, had the potential to become a fully developed industrial power. Moreover, Iran's oil reserves were much smaller than Saudi Arabia's and he saw economic diversification not only as possible but necessary, and that it must be achieved as fast as possible. His development programme, which had begun with the White Revolution in 1963, had clearly followed such an approach. In his book *The White Revolution*, the Shah wrote:

> The revolutionary aim which I have presented to my people, to which my people have responded with decisiveness and clarity, is that, God willing, I should utilize the present opportunity to construct a modern and progressive Iran on sound and strong foundations, so that my presence should no longer affect the destiny of the country. For inevitably I will go sooner or later, while Iran and its society will remain. It is therefore my duty to try to ensure during my lifetime that this society will become as prosperous and secure as possible.[40]

The Shah's development plans were greatly expanded in the 1970s as oil revenues increased due to the energy crisis. Among his new schemes were huge development projects such as the expansion of the Bandar Abbas seaport, and the construction of the trans-Turkey oil pipeline which would give Iran better access to European markets.[41]

To pay for these ambitious schemes, the Shah pursued a policy of demanding sharp increases in Iran's OPEC quotas for oil production as well as sharp increases in the price. Iranian policies suffered, however, because of his inflated view of the importance of Iranian interests. In his view, Iran had greater needs than other Gulf oil-producing countries, including Saudi Arabia, and he thought that they should agree to lower production quotas and consequently lower revenues in order to maintain high prices. Moreover, the Shah was spending huge sums on expanding his armed forces, sums that could only be justified in terms of his imperial ambitions. Thus his inflexibility on OPEC price and production rates was in great part the result of his own arrogance and ambition.[42]

Saudi Arabia adopted a very different policy. King Faisal's aim was to 'balance the interests' of all oil-producing countries. Such a policy was based on maintaining a gradual rise in oil prices and sensible control over production. It aimed at respecting the interests of the oil-consuming nations, particularly those of the Third World which could not sustain a sharp rise in oil prices. King Faisal also believed that a precipitous price rise would lead to a sharp increase in the prices of imported goods and materials from the industrial nations, especially since many of the oil-producing countries were dependent on foreign imports.

In operational terms, the Kingdom of Saudi Arabia sought through its leadership of OPEC to maintain a stable and gradual rise in oil prices. Its decision to be a founding member of OPEC was based on the conviction that a collective policy by all oil-producing countries would serve the interests of both producers and consumers. Moderate and stable prices, in the Saudi view, made for a healthier world economy. As the Kingdom saw it, if the world economy sank, Saudi Arabia would sink with it. Economic chaos would be followed by political chaos, either from the far left or the far right. Thus Saudi Arabia used its leadership position in OPEC to try to keep stable, moderate prices and, in so doing, often came into direct confrontation with Iran.

The Saudi policy on moderate prices also conformed to its domestic economic interests. With huge oil reserves, but few human and natural resources other than oil, the Kingdom needed to be able to maintain a long-term oil market. It feared that if prices were too high, consumers would be encouraged to develop non-oil energy sources and deprive all OPEC members of their major export.

King Faisal objected to the Shah's hawkish price policies for political as well as economic reasons. He felt that the Shah, in pursuing his own grandiose ambitions, was disregarding the interests of other OPEC members. The Shah's arrogance, moreover, was in the King's view greatly strengthened by almost unlimited American support for Iran's military expansion plans. King Faisal felt the United States should work to persuade the Shah to accept price restraint and respect the OPEC production quota.

Bilateral relations deteriorated further in 1973, when the Shah refused to join Saudi Arabia and the other Arab oil-producing countries in enforcing an oil embargo against the consuming countries which supported Israel during the 1967 Arab–Israeli war. Ignoring the embargo, the Shah continued to supply Israel with oil, seeing no link between politics and economics in this case. He claimed that the oil was an 'economic commodity' rather than an 'economic weapon' and, therefore, it should not be used to achieve political goals.

At the same time, the Shah manipulated the temporary oil shortage created by the embargo to win another oil price rise at the December 1973 OPEC meeting, quadrupling the price from the previous September and precipitating the world energy crisis. The prices were too high for the world economy and by the middle of 1974, a world recession resulted. Realizing that he had miscalculated, the Shah started hinting that Iran might moderate its position in the interest of world economic stability and would like to rebuild its political and economic relations with Saudi Arabia and the rest of the Arab world.

This change in attitude encouraged Saudi Arabia to reappraise its relations with Iran and once again seek closer co-operation on oil and other economic policies. On 15 October 1974 the Saudi Minister of State for Foreign Affairs, accompanied by Prince Saud al-Faisal, then Deputy Oil Minister, visited Tehran and met with the Shah to discuss oil prices and related issues.[43] The visit was followed by a meeting in France between Prince Fahd ibn Abd al-Aziz, then Minister of the Interior and Deputy Prime Minister, and Iran's Minister of Finance and the Economy, where they discussed the same issues. The meetings were constructive and the two countries began to seek new ways of co-operation. Although the meetings did not immediately result in lowering oil prices, they did pave the way for closer bilateral relations.

As a result of this new Saudi-Iranian *rapprochement*, trade relations were resumed (although they had not formally been cut off). Iranian non-oil exports to the Kingdom in 1974 rose to IR 560,927 (US$1 = IR60) and the number of Iranian *hajjis* increased in 1974 to 40,000 from 24,000 in the previous year.[44] In another clear sign of its willingness to co-operate more closely with Iran and rebuild the relationship, Saudi Arabia decided in 1974 to elevate its diplomatic representation in Tehran from a *chargé d'affaires* to an ambassador.[45]

When King Faisal was assassinated in 1975, the transition of power to King Khalid and Crown Prince Fahd was smooth and did not impair Saudi foreign relations, including those with Iran. Until the overthrow of the Iranian monarchy in 1979, Saudi-Iranian economic, including oil, relations remained cordial.

Saudi-Iranian co-operation on oil policies reached a high point in 1977, when the Shah finally abandoned his hawkish price policies. During a state visit to the United States in November 1977, the Shah pledged to President Jimmy Carter that Iran would oppose precipitous oil price increases in future OPEC meetings.[46] Prior to that, on 13 July 1977, the Iranian delegation to the OPEC Stockholm meeting had agreed with the Saudi delegation that both countries should consider an oil-price freeze through 1978. The Kingdom had also agreed at that time to purchase Iranian crude for its own refineries. The Shah's pledge was a victory for Saudi Arabia's oil policies, which had always aimed at balancing the interests of producers and consumers through the maintenance of steady, low prices.

Saudi-Iranian economic relations took an abrupt turn for the worse on 16 January 1979 when the Shah was forced to flee Iran and his regime was toppled in a revolution led by the ayatollahs. On 1 February 1979 the

Economic Relations 1932–82

spiritual leader of the Iranian revolution, Ayatollah Khomeini, arrived in Tehran to establish a new regime. Despite reservations, the Kingdom of Saudi Arabia recognized the new government and expressed its willingness to continue co-operating with Iran on all levels. For its part, the new regime indicated that Iran would limit oil production and seek higher prices, a policy that would oblige Saudi Arabia to try to hold other OPEC countries in line to keep prices from soaring. None the less in 1979 oil prices jumped from $18 to $28 a barrel as the oil market reacted to the downfall of the Shah and the success of the revolution in Iran. However, the world market, which was already in decline, could not sustain the jump in prices and soon resumed its downward turn. Consequently, a confrontation between Saudi Arabia and the new regime in Iran over oil prices was averted more by the market than by Iranian policies.

Overall bilateral relations deteriorated, however, and reached an unprecedented state of animosity with the outbreak of the Iran–Iraq war in September 1980. Economic relations were further undermined as the war began to grind down the Iranian economy to an extent that it has not yet recovered. Moreover, oil relations were largely put on hold as a result of the oil glut and Iran's inability to affect the market one way or another. The new regime none the less continued to allow *hajjis* to travel to the Kingdom; indeed, many of those posing as *hajjis* were really agents of the Iranian government seeking to foment trouble in order to embarrass the Kingdom in the eyes of the Muslim *ummah*. They distributed anti-Saudi propaganda and pro-Iranian pamphlets and pictures of Khomeini, and even attempted acts of sabotage. Nevertheless, the Kingdom continued to allow Iranians to make the *hajj* in conformity with its sacred responsibility for this act of faith.

The combination of the near collapse of the Iranian economy as a result of the Iran–Iraq war and government mismanagement, and the extension of the oil glut, together with still strained political relations, suggests that an improvement in Saudi-Iranian economic relations will be very slow in coming. Looking back over the last 70 years, this is not unusual. The course of economic relations has been erratic, full of ups and downs, and will probably continue to be so.

6
Military Relations 1932–82

No book on Middle East politics is complete without reference to the military aspects of the region. Since the beginning of recorded history, the Middle East has been a battleground—between tribes, between states and between empires. Moreover, Middle Eastern conflicts have a tendency to escalate as the combatants call on the loyalty and self-interest of their neighbours. This tendency is illustrated in the old tribal maxim, 'My brother and I against my cousin, my cousin and I against the stranger.' Another maxim illustrates the tendency of interstate wars to escalate: 'The enemy of my enemy is my friend, and the friend of my enemy is my enemy.' The development of independent nation-states, particularly in the aftermath of the Second World War, has greatly expanded the scope for regional armed conflict, as rival states have striven for strong armies and military supremacy.

Middle Eastern wars, ancient and modern, have been fought over territorial claims, natural resources such as water, and for political reaons. Some of the greatest motivating factors, however, are nationalist, ethnic and religious rivalries. In both World Wars and in the Cold War, the Middle East region was also deeply involved, directly and indirectly, in the military rivalries of outside powers. Thus military relationships cannot be ignored when writing about the Middle East.

Both Saudi Arabia and Iran have strong military traditions. Riza Shah and King Abd al-Aziz used military force to reunite their countries and create modern states, although the means and tactics were different. Riza Shah used modern warfare, whereas Abd al-Aziz's Muslim army was made up of traditional desert warriors. In addition, the objectives of the two rulers were different. Abd al-Aziz sought to unite Arabia as an Islamic state under the banner of the Unitarian (Wahhabi) revival, while Riza Shah sought to create a modern, secular state with power concentrated in his own hands.

In uniting Arabia, the then Amir Abd al-Aziz first had to recapture his Najdi homeland from the Al Rashids who had expelled his father in the late nineteenth century. With only 40 brave, fearless and loyal fighters, he retook the Saudi capital Riyadh in 1902. Over the next 30 years, he gradually expanded his control to include most of present-day Saudi Arabia. The expansion was accomplished by his desert forces, the Ikhwan (the Brethren). The King fostered and supported the Ikhwan movement in the early 1900s. It first appeared in the vicinity of Riyadh, where it was soon regarded with fear by many tribes.

In its early days, members of the movement were drawn from three major tribes, the Mutayr, the Utaybah and the Harb. A smaller number of Ikhwan came from the Dawasir and the Subai' tribes.[1] The leading spirit behind the movement was Faisal al-Dawish, Sheikh of the Mutayr. The movement fervently adhered to the Wahhabi Islamic reform movement and was dedicated to purifying Islam of the many corrupt practices that had crept into it since the time of the Prophet Muhammad. The Ikhwan grew into a force that, at its strongest, numbered between 5,000 and 6,000 men. Its ultimate test was the defeat of Sharif Hussein of Makkah and the conquest of the Hijaz, completed in 1926. As both the Ikhwan and the King's dominions expanded, he appointed his eldest sons, Princes Saud, Faisal and Muhammad, as unit commanders of the Ikhwan. King Faisal led in the capture of Jeddah and Prince Muhammad in the capture of Madinah.

The unification of Najd, the Eastern Province, the Hijaz and Asir culminated in the creation of the Kingdom of Saudi Arabia in 1932, completing a 30-year process which had begun in 1902. With the unification complete, King Abd al-Aziz disbanded the Ikhwan. In 1934, however, the King and his eldest sons, Saud and Faisal, were to raise an army including many Ikhwan veterans for a brief war with Yemen. As a result, the 1934 border treaty between Saudi Arabia and Yemen was signed. This treaty is still valid and constitutes the basis for the current unofficial border between the two countries.

With the vast size of his territories, King Abd al-Aziz was concerned for the military security of his people; in the 1930s he created a Defence Agency to replace the Ikhwan. In 1944 he elevated it to full ministry status and appointed one of his sons, Prince Mansur ibn Abd al-Aziz, to be the first minister. The task of the ministry was to create and maintain a modern defence force. That is still the primary mission of the present-day Ministry of Defence, headed by Prince Sultan ibn Abd al-Aziz, who is also Second Deputy Prime Minister.

To augment the regular armed forces, the King reconstituted his desert forces in the 1940s. At first called the White Army because of their white *thobs* (robes), they are the present-day National Guard, under the command of Crown Prince Abdallah ibn Abd al-Aziz.

Iran, on the other hand, had a modern military establishment already in place prior to the country's unification by Riza Khan. A military officer in the Persian army who took advantage of the deteriorating political situation in Persia in 1921 to move against Tehran, the political capital of the Qajar dynasty, in a bloodless coup, Riza Khan was then able to manipulate the civilian government and the Majlis to consolidate his power. He also conquered a number of small neighbouring provinces such as Arabistan. In 1925 he ousted the last Qajar Shah and became absolute monarch. As a man with military experience, Riza Shah appreciated the role of a strong military force, not only in national defence but as a foreign-policy tool, through the use of intimidation. During his reign and afterwards, Iran had many border disputes with its neighbours, and Riza Shah made a strong armed force one of his top priorities. He also saw the need for strong security forces to maintain domestic stability and quell public reaction to his dictatorial rule.

From this brief historical overview, two conclusions can be drawn. First, the military establishment of Iran during the 1920s and 1930s was much more organized and developed than that of Saudi Arabia. Second, whereas King Abd al-Aziz perceived military power as a means to unify and defend his country, Riza Shah saw it as a means to consolidate his personal power and, if possible, extend Iran's power as far beyond the country's borders as possible. In other words, the Shah's desire for military power was far more confrontational than that of the King, who sought national security more through co-operation. With this in mind, we can examine and analyse the military relations between the two countries in two contexts, confrontation and co-operation. We should bear in mind, however, that both confrontation and co-operation in military relations are basically products of national security interests as perceived by a country's leaders. They are thus not only closely related, but are in many respects sides of the same coin.

Saudi–Iranian Relations 1932–1982

Confrontational Issues

Reference to confrontation is not intended to imply that the two countries, Saudi Arabia and Iran, have engaged directly in military conflict. Indeed, no direct military confrontation of any significance has occurred between troops of Iran and those of the Arabian peninsula since AD 645, when the Arab Muslim armies conquered Persia in response to the orders of the second Caliph, Omar ibn al-Khattab. Even during the recent Iraq–Iran war (1980–88), during which Saudi Arabia was obliged to support Iraq as a sister Arab country, no serious military confrontation between Saudi Arabia and Iran took place.

The potential for confrontation between Saudi Arabia and Iran has occurred during the past 70 years over a number of issues, particularly those involving territorial claims, as will be examined below.

Arabistan

The first such issue arose in April 1925, when Riza Shah brutally conquered the principality of Arabistan, which was under an Arab ruler, Sheikh Khaz'al. The subjugation of an Arab sheikhdom under Persian rule was a matter of deep concern for King Abd al-Aziz. He was in no position to challenge Riza Shah due to the fact that he himself was, at the time, engaged in unifying his own country. Realizing that Riza Shah was an ambitious man and that, were the British to relinquish their protective status over other Gulf sheikhdoms such as Bahrain or even Kuwait, the Shah would seize any favourable opportunity to use military force to subjugate them as well, the King took the decisive act of signing a bilateral treaty with the British government in 1927, recognizing the governments of Bahrain, Kuwait, Qatar and Oman, and their protective treaties with the British Empire.[2]

King Abd al-Aziz hoped to reassure them that he himself did not intend to invade them, but, on the contrary, wanted to guarantee their territorial integrity from Riza Shah's jingoistic and expansionist policies. He also wanted to send an indirect message to Riza Shah that the latter's territorial ambitions could not be tolerated and must cease. For his part, Riza Shah viewed the Saudi–British treaty as a challenge to his country's claim over Bahrain. He immediately sent his diplomatic representative in Cairo to King Abd al-Aziz with a 'memorandum of objection' to the treaty and demanding the return of Bahrain to Persia's domain.[3] The Shah also lodged an official complaint with the League of Nations, asking that British protection over Bahrain be removed and the island be returned to Persian sovereignty.[4]

The Saudi government responded decisively to the Persian claim by sending a memorandum to the British Legation in Jeddah stating that:

The government of the Kingdom of Arabia knows nothing about Iran's rights in Bahrain. This is the first time we have received a memorandum containing such kind of claim. Despite the fact that Bahrain belonged in the past to the grandfathers of King Abd al-Aziz ibn Saud, the Saudi government has recognized Muhammad ibn Issa as the Amir of Bahrain, and signed an agreement with Bahrain, taking into consideration that Bahrain's ruler is Hamad ibn Issa.[5]

Bahrain and the Gulf Islands Dispute
Iran's claim to sovereignty over Bahrain was another source of political and potential military confrontation between the two countries; it was to remain a cause of great concern in the Gulf region for a number of decades. The historical basis of Iran's claim over Bahrain was simply that it has a large Shi'a population. Riza Shah resurrected the claim during his reign, but so long as the British maintained their protective status over the sheikhdom, the issue was little more than a nuisance in Saudi–Iranian relations. During the Second World War, when Riza Shah was forced to abdicate and Iran was occupied by Allied forces, the Bahrain issue was temporarily forgotten. But following the war, Muhammad Riza Shah again revived Iran's claim to Bahrain. In the Iranian Majlis, two seats were even reserved for 'representatives' of Bahrain.

The territorial claim became the subject of the first meeting between the heads of state of Saudi Arabia and Iran, which took place in August 1955 when King Saud visited Tehran.[6] Although the talks were very cordial, no conclusive decisions were taken on how to resolve the dispute. In 1957 the issue was raised again during the Shah's official visit to Saudi Arabia, but again the two monarchs could not reach a solution. They agreed, implicitly, to let the United Nations deal with the issue.[7]

For the next decade, Iran's claim to Bahrain continued to sour its relations with the Gulf Arab states. Matters came to a head in 1968 when Britain announced its intention to relinquish its protective status in the Gulf by 1971. The British realized that before they withdrew, they must seek to resolve the territorial disputes between Iran and the Gulf sheikhdoms. With international support, they persuaded the United Nations to create a commission to review and settle the Bahrain issue.

Throughout this period, the Saudis tried to promote co-operation and seek an amicable resolution to the Iranian territorial claims. Nevertheless, neither the efforts of the King or the United Nations nor private mediation initially succeeded in convincing the Shah to drop his claim over Bahrain. Finally, during the Shah's second visit to Saudi Arabia in November 1968, King Faisal succeeded in persuading him to abandon his claim and allow the UN committee to conduct its investigative mission to determine where sovereignty lay. The King had raised the issue with the Shah in view of a number of statements made by the Shah and other Iranian politicians as early as April 1968, when they began to state privately that they had little interest in Bahrain. The issue was finally resolved in late 1970, when the Shah accepted the UN finding that Bahrain should be a sovereign state. Thus, when the British withdrew early the following year, Bahrain became a fully independent state.

Although he agreed to give up his claim to Bahrain, the Shah was determined that Iran should not lose face. His strategy was to reassert Iran's territorial claim to three small islands in the lower Gulf owned by two of the Trucial States, now the United Arab Emirates.[8] Abu Musa was owned by Sharjah and Greater Tunb and Lesser Tunb were owned by Ras al-Khaymah. The rulers of these two sheikhdoms were members of the Qawasim tribe, which at one time in history had also ruled on the Persian side of the Strait of Hormuz where they were suzerain to the Persian Shahs. On this basis, Muhammad Riza Shah reasoned that the Qasimi islands belonged to Iran.[9] Moreover, by claiming them, Iran could also lay claim to any oil found in their territorial waters.

During the visit to Saudi Arabia in April 1970 by Iran's Prime Minister and Foreign Minister Ardashir Zahedi, the two countries agreed in principle that the Gulf region should be kept stable and peaceful. During the meeting, the Kingdom advised Iran to moderate its claim over the islands and suggested that if security (rather than sovereignty) were the issue, some joint Iranian–Arab force might be stationed on the islands.[10] Having 'lost' Bahrain, however, the Shah was determined to claim the islands. Harry Kern, editor of *Foreign Reports Bulletin* and a long-time observer of Gulf affairs, recalled that period in an interview in Washington in the autumn of 1991:

> I recollect quite vividly going to see King Faisal at the time when the Iranians made their decision to occupy the two Tunbs and Abu Musa and told the King what was about to happen. Faisal's reaction was one of fairly complete surprise. While we talked, he pressed a button and ordered somebody to find out more about the islands. I remember, shortly after the occupation, Alam, then Minister of Court, told me that the Iranians were armed only with flint guns to bat the flies on Abu Musa. At one point, half-way into the island, some emissaries appeared from Sharjah and said: 'What are you doing, these are Sharjah flies!'[11]

Iran occupied the three islands on 30 November 1971. Contrary to what the Iranian Minister of Court had told Kern, Iran deployed naval forces, air force helicopters, and a large number of army troops and officers to take over the islands. Indeed, it was a show of force. The Saudi reaction was one of outrage. In view of all their efforts aimed at avoiding a military confrontation with Iran over the Gulf islands, and to solve the issue peacefully, and in view of Iran's acceptance of these Saudi initiatives, the Iranian invasion came as quite a shock to the Saudi leadership. It resulted in a grievous setback for Saudi–Iranian relations and prompted the two countries to embark on an arms race. In mid-1972, for example, the Shah decided to purchase 750–800 British Chieftain tanks, 140 F-4 Phantom jets, 4 frigates, 3 destroyers plus large numbers of other arms such as F-5 and C-130 transport planes.[12]

This arms deal was clear evidence that the Shah envisaged an ever greater role for Iran not only in the Gulf region but extending throughout the Indian Ocean. Saudi Arabia was ultimately obliged to follow suit. Thus in 1973 and 1974 the Kingdom took steps to strengthen its air force capabilities by acquiring more F-5Es and F-5Fs and to upgrade its air defence programme with more sophisticated Hawk surface-to-air missiles.[13] The Kingdom also sought broader military co-operation with neighbouring Arab Gulf states. In March 1973 the Saudi Defence Minister, Prince Sultan ibn Abd al-Aziz, toured the Gulf states, visiting the Sultanate of Oman, Qatar and Bahrain. The purpose of the tour was to discuss defence matters and to organize closer co-operation between Saudi Arabia and those states.

The Median Line Dispute
One of the most troublesome issues in the Gulf region in modern times has been the determination of the Median Line, the demarcation of offshore oil rights for the riparian states. Throughout the negotiation of the Median Line, Iran was particularly difficult, always seeking to gain advantage at the cost of the other states. Saudi–Iranian negotiations were no exception.

In 1965 the two countries came close to a military confrontation over the Median Line. After difficult negotiations, they finally agreed in 1966 to establish a committee of experts to examine the issue and submit its recommendations for delineating the Median Line between the two countries. After two years, the committee came up with its recommendations for drawing the line. It also recommended the two countries share oil revenues from certain wells that were located right on the line.

The recommendations were presented to the leaders of the two countries at a summit meeting in Saudi Arabia in 1968 where they both signed the final agreement on the issue. The agreement also resolved a territorial dispute over two small Gulf islands, Arabi and Farsi, whereby Saudi Arabia was given full control over Arabi and Iran over Farsi. The agreement thus ended what had long been one of the most confrontational issues between the two countries.

In addition to these territorial disputes, two broader security issues played an important role in Saudi-Iranian military relations, the Arab-Israeli problem and Gulf security.

The Arab-Israeli Problem
Soon after the creation of Israel in 1948, Iran granted it *de facto* recognition. This act greatly damaged Iran's relations with all the Arab states. Saudi Arabia, however, did not want an open confrontation with Iran on this issue, hoping that one day Iran would realize that its relations with the Arab world were much more important than those with Israel. Nevertheless, the Kingdom noted with great concern Iran's links with Israel, particularly in the military field.

In the early 1960s the Kingdom received information from confidential sources in Paris that the Shah planned to give all the repair and maintenance work on Iran's recently acquired F-5 planes to the Israelis through the Israeli Military Industries.[14] The news alarmed Saudi authorities and had the Shah gone through with it, it could have done irrefutable damage to Iranian relations with all the Arab states, including Saudi Arabia. Perhaps the Shah became aware of the potential unpleasant consequences, for he ultimately decided not to give the maintenance contract to the Israelis. In so doing, he avoided what could well have been a break in relations with Saudi Arabia and all the other Arab states.

Ten years later, Iran and Israel began talks on a similar project, but on a much wider scale. The two countries were conducting discussions on setting up the largest aircraft repair and maintenance centre in the Middle East, to be based in Tehran. The project provided for an investment of $30 million and the employment of several hundred Israeli technicians. This time, Iran's Foreign Minister, Ardashir Zahedi, persuaded the Shah to drop the idea because of the catastrophic consequences it would have on Iran's relations with the Arab world.[15]

In both cases, the Kingdom was alarmed for three simple reasons. First, its own relationship with Iran would suffer. Second, Iran would be more isolated in the Gulf region as well as in the Arab world. Third, Iran did not need such close ties with the Israelis since its military ties with the United States were quite sufficient. Nevertheless, the collapse of both projects was a relief for Saudi Arabia and a disappointment for the Israelis.

Military Relations 1932-82

Gulf Regional Security
Gulf regional security was an external issue long before it was an issue among the Gulf states themselves. For centuries, European imperial powers had competed with each other for commercial and political concessions in the region, with the balance of power shifting as one or another of those countries gained or lost influence. Iran was particularly vulnerable to foreign imperialism, with Russia steadily moving south, in search, it has been suggested, of a 'warm water port', and Britain moving north and west from its imperial stronghold in India. During the Second World War, the armies of these two countries occupied practically the whole of Iran and forced Riza Shah off the throne for his pro-German sympathies. Saudi Arabia, on the other hand, had a quite different experience. Whereas the British created a protectorate and a crown colony of Aden in southern Yemen, and had a protective status over the Gulf sheikhdoms and Oman, the Kingdom never experienced the imperialist policies of the Western powers, and was hence able to deal with the West far more objectively than most of its neighbours. At the end of the Second World War, Saudi Arabia was the only Gulf country to be totally independent of any foreign political or military influence.

Following the war and lasting up to the end of the Cold War, the Western powers were particularly concerned with containing the southward Soviet expansion. The Soviets had already tried to create a Soviet Republic of Gilan in 1920-21, and tried in 1945-46 to create 'autonomous republics' in Azerbaijan and among the Kurds in Mahabad. To meet the Soviet threat, the United States developed a containment policy and tried to create alliances around the world to stop the Soviets. In the Middle East, it tried to create a Middle East Defence Organization, naively believing that Arabs would join with Israel to fight communism. When that did not work out, the Americans encouraged the regional states and Britain to form a pact.

Accordingly, Britain, Iraq, Iran, Turkey and Pakistan entered into a military pact which was signed in Baghdad on 24 February 1955 and became known as the Baghdad Pact. The United States joined the pact only as an observer. Nevertheless, the pact was viewed with hostility by a number of Arab countries, including the Kingdom of Saudi Arabia, which believed that it was aimed at dividing the Arab world and conspiring against those newly established Arab revolutionary regimes that had established ties with Moscow. Consequently, the pact became a confrontational issue between Saudi Arabia and Iran.

The tripartite military attack on Egypt in 1956 by Britain, France and Israel greatly strengthened Saudi feelings against the Baghdad Pact, especially since Britain, one of the states attacking Egypt, was a member of the pact. Thus, when the Shah visited Saudi Arabia in 1957, the issue was raised by King Saud, who made it clear to the Shah that he was very suspicious of the pact's aims and would like to see Iran out of it. The Shah, on the other hand, defended the pact and its goals and even argued that it would enhance security and stability in the Gulf region.

In 1958 a military coup overthrew the Hashimite monarchy in Iraq, and the new republican government withdrew from the alliance.[16] Renamed the Central Treaty Organization (CENTO), it no longer had any Arab members and concerned itself solely with the Soviet threat from the north, and ultimately faded into oblivion.

Due to the British presence in the region as protectors of the sheikhdoms and guarantor of security of the Gulf, neither Saudi Arabia nor the Gulf sheikhdoms felt the same degree of concern over the Soviet threat as did Iran. In 1968, however, when Britain announced its plan to withdraw militarily from the region by the end of 1971, Saudi Arabia and the small sheikhdoms were alarmed, not just over the Soviet threat and that of revolutionary Iraq, which worried the Western powers, but over Iranian intentions, particularly in view of Iran's military build-up and its potential expansionist policies.

Indeed, the Iranian threat was a major catalyst for the creation of the Gulf Co-operation Council in 1981. The GCC was created to co-ordinate the social, political and economic policies of the Gulf states as well as for military co-operation. But greater military co-operation was definitely a goal. Early on, the Kingdom submitted a 'Gulf Collective Security' proposal to the GCC countries which envisaged an independent military force for each GCC member and encouraged them to strengthen their armies' fighting capabilities. Building on that, the Saudi proposal ultimately envisioned a GCC rapid deployment force that could be used in times of emergency.

The strategic importance of Gulf oil, and the potential Soviet and radical Arab threat, had made the maintenance of security and stability in the region a high priority issue on the American international strategy agenda. This priority was reflected in 1969 when President Nixon announced what became known as the 'Nixon Doctrine', in which he referred to the security of the Gulf region. He called for close ties between the United States and the Gulf countries, particularly Saudi Arabia and Iran. This position was later to become known as the 'Twin Pillar Policy'. Although the Americans never understood the limits of Iranian-Arab co-operation, or why the Gulf Arabs felt as threatened by the Iranians as by the Soviets, the policy succeeded in meeting the required level of security against the Soviet threat in the region at the time. Moreover, the US felt that by strengthening its co-operation with these two countries, it no longer needed to think of establishing military bases in the area.

Contrary to the fears of many, the Soviet Union did not attempt to fill a power vacuum believed to be created by the departing British. This was so for several reasons. First, the world energy shortage of the 1970s demonstrated to the Soviets how vital the region had become for the Western world, and they did not want to risk a global war arising out of a confrontation there. Their initial policy approach, therefore, was a policy of 'accommodation and proxies', whereby they tried to establish diplomatic relations with the newly independent sheikhdoms, and also support their allies in the area such as South Yemen. As a result, their attitude at the time was cautious and calculating, in sharp contrast to the atmosphere in the early 1960s when Soviet Premier Khrushchev proclaimed that Iran would fall into Russian hands like a ripe apple.

Such threats to the Gulf region in particular, and the Middle East in general, led Saudi Arabia and Iran to broad agreement on a number of principles:

1. The need to keep the Gulf region out of the superpowers' armed conflicts.
2. The need to ensure that foreign military bases were not established in the Gulf region.
3. The need for the Gulf states to build their own military power in order to defend themselves.
4. The need for a collective security arrangement in the Gulf region.
5. The need for all Gulf countries to maintain a reliable internal security force that could enforce law and order and deal effectively with any domestic threat.
6. The need to combat all kinds of terrorism by all possible means.
7. The need to stand against all radical and extremist groups and movements that aimed at disturbing the security and stability in the region in particular and the Middle East in general.

With this kind of understanding between the two countries, they were able to contain many of the potential problems and deal effectively with them.

A second reason for caution in the region was the Iranian revolution of 1979. The new militant Shi'a regime was violently anti-Western, but was equally anti-communist. When the Iran–Iraq war broke out the following year, the Soviets found themselves, along with the Americans and Saudi Arabia, supporting Iraq to prevent its being defeated. The Iran–Iraq war grew out of the confrontational attitude adopted by the new revolutionary regime in Tehran towards all its neighbours, including Saudi Arabia. When all-out war broke out in September 1980, the Kingdom had no choice but to support Iraq, a fellow Arab state, due to the hostile attitude of the new regime in Iran towards Saudi Arabia and the other Gulf states. In his talk to the scholars and Muslim country representatives who attended the Jihad Festival sponsored by Imam Muhammad ibn Saud University in Riyadh (18–20 February 1991), the Custodian of the Two Holy Mosques, King Fahd ibn Abd al-Aziz, said in this regard:

> Allah knows that when we helped Iraq, the intention was not to harm any country, and I refer here to Iran, but the primary aim was to preserve Iraq. It is widely known that Iraq cannot occupy Iran... As I said before, we do not want to make trouble for Iran or harm it, but we also do not want Iraq to be occupied by any country because it is an Arab country and a neighbour.[17]

King Fahd's words were a clear statement that Saudi Arabia's policy towards Iran, particularly when it comes to military affairs, was to seek peace and harmony. The Kingdom never intended to harm Iran or its people and never looked upon Iran as a hostile country. On the contrary, the Kingdom viewed Iran as a Muslim sister country which, as such, should be an asset to the Islamic world.

Despite all these efforts, Saudi Arabia and Iran continued to search for security and stability in the Gulf region in accordance with their national interests. Contrary to many beliefs, the Shah had never considered controlling the Gulf, although he certainly planned to project military power into the Arabian Sea through various bases he had built, such as the Shah Bahar base. In the meantime, it became clear in the mid-1970s that the Shah's motives in obtaining more and more weapons sprang, first, from the desire to acquire such arms and, second, to exert authority in the Gulf and beyond. Acting as the Gulf 'policeman' was a well-known strategy of Shah Muhammad Riza Pahlavi.

Co-operation Issues

The confrontational issues in Saudi–Iranian military relations mentioned above do not mean that the two countries have had no positive and co-operative military relations. On the contrary, the two countries were able to find mutual grounds for military co-operation in a number of areas. Their mutual interests in seeking security and stability in the Gulf region in particular, and their search for peace and stability in the Middle East in general, both led to successful efforts in military co-operation.

The idea of military co-operation between Saudi Arabia and Iran goes back to 1929, when King Abd al-Aziz proposed a defence pact between the two countries. Riza Shah, however, decided not to pursue the idea, preferring to go his own way in building Iran's military strength. During the 1930s, events leading up to the Second World War dominated the political and military spectrum of the region and there was no common ground for bilateral military co-operation. When war broke out, Saudi Arabia unhesitatingly sided with the Allies. US–Saudi military relations were formally initiated on 18 February 1943, when the US government declared the Kingdom eligible for American Lend–Lease aid.[18] Saudi–British military co-operation began at about the same time.

Iran began the war supporting the Axis powers. Indeed, it was mainly for this reason that the Allies forced Riza Shah to abdicate in favour of his son, Muhammad Riza Pahlavi. The accession of Shah Muhammad Riza Pahlavi was a major turning-point for Iranian military development. As time passed, the Shah became increasingly dependent on American military technology and weapons systems, particularly after 1953 when he was reinstalled by the United States as Iran's absolute monarch, following the Mossadeq crisis. Consequently, in March 1959 an American–Iranian military treaty was signed. An American military base was accordingly built in Iran, and American weapons and training teams began arriving in the country.[19]

The post-Second World War era witnessed a growing role for both Saudi Arabia and Iran in Western strategic planning. They were considered to be the most important countries in the Gulf region, both geographically and as major oil producers. Thus, it was in the interest of the Western powers to see that these two countries co-operated and achieved sound internal security and political stability, particularly in the case of Iran which went through a period of political unrest during the Mossadeq years.

In view of these interests, one could argue that the concept of Saudi–Iranian co-operation underlaid the American 'Twin Pillar Policy' of the 1970s, and had actually been operating since the 1940s. It could also be argued that Iraq had been an important regional military power to the West in the 1940s, but that, following the revolution of 1958, it had become a revolutionary state with close ties to the Soviet Union, denouncing the West and its presence in the region.

The mutual Saudi and Iranian interest in halting the spread of revolutionary and communist influence in the region does not mean that the two countries fought wars together or entered into a military allliance. But they did, from time to time, attempt to reach a common understanding on a number of related military issues bearing on their mutual security.

The 1957 Proposed Military Pact

As mentioned above, the idea of a bilateral military pact was first proposed by King Abd al-Aziz during the first official visit of its kind by a Saudi delegation to Tehran in 1929. The King envisaged an alliance under which each country would materially help the other in case of military attack by a third party. Shah Riza Pahlavi, however, preferred only a Treaty of Friendship, which was signed in Tehran during the visit.

The idea of a defence pact was next raised by Shah Muhammad Riza Pahlavi during an official visit to Saudi Arabia in 1957. The Kingdom was not unsympathetic to the idea this time, and in the final communiqué, the two countries agreed to discuss the matter further.[20] In the end, however, no military treaty was signed. At the time, the proposal was seen by many Middle Eastern experts as a tactical move by the Shah to isolate Saudi Arabia from Egypt and Syria.[21] The British suspected the idea as aimed more against them. R.B. Stevens, the British representative in Tehran, reported to his government on the issue:

> There is material here for closer working arrangements—whether or not these lead to the sort of 'bilateral defence pact' about which the Shah has been...thinking and which I understand he discussed with my United States colleague before leaving to Riyadh... But I cannot help suspecting that something more than the obvious advantages which meet the eye has played a part in his idea of a bilateral defence pact. What does seem fairly obvious is that, whatever the Shah's intentions may be, a close working arrangement between Iran and Saudi Arabia would eventually bring both countries up against the problem of the British-protected Sheikhdoms in the Gulf.[22]

In essence, the British representative in Tehran was not asking his government to oppose outright the defence pact between Saudi Arabia and Iran, but only expressing his suspicion of the idea. In this regard his telegram continued:

> In conclusion, to the present, I submit that we should not oppose, but should, on the contrary, discreetly encourage, closer relationships between Iran and Saudi Arabia. We should show interest in, and keenly watch the development of, any idea of a bilateral defence pact.[23]

The British suspicions could be attributed to the fact that Saudi Arabia and Britain were not on good terms at the time: diplomatic relations between them had been broken off as a result of British participation in the tripartite attack on Egypt in 1956.

The 1962 Yemen Civil War

In September 1962 an Egyptian-sponsored coup took place in North Yemen, on the southern borders of Saudi Arabia, that overthrew the monarchy and replaced it with a revolutionary republican regime. Both King Faisal of Saudi Arabia and the Shah of Iran were alarmed, for Egyptian President Nasser had clearly embarked on a policy of seeking to overthrow all monarchies in the Middle East. The Yemeni republicans, however, failed to capture the Imam, Muhammad al-Badr, who escaped to the northern part of Yemen where he began to organize the fight to regain his throne. In order to do so, he needed Saudi assistance and whatever help he could get from other countries. For Saudi Arabia, the decision to support the Imam was a difficult one. The Kingdom did not want to interfere in the internal policies of its neighbour or, indeed, of any Arab country. However, the Yemeni coup was not only against the Imam, but was a personal challenge by President Nasser against Saudi Arabia—a challenge that had to be met.

Thus the Kingdom extended its help to the Imam and encouraged other countries to do likewise. The Shah's initial reaction was to wait and see. But in 1964, as the conflict between the republican regime (backed by Egypt) and the Yemeni royalists (backed by Saudi Arabia, Jordan and Morocco) dragged on and turned into a bloody civil war, the Shah decided to assist the royalists. Although he never sent troops, he assisted with arms, supplies and military training. The latter was conducted inside Iran where Yemeni troops were transported from Saudi Arabia to Iranian military bases. At the time, this co-operation was seen as a clear sign of willingness on the part of the Shah to co-ordinate with Saudi Arabia on military matters that affected their mutual security.

The Dhufar Rebellion in Oman

By 1960 several groups of anti-regime rebels had been operating in the Sultanate of Oman, particularly in its westernmost Dhufar province, for a number of years. The creation of a Marxist regime in South Yemen in 1968 gave the rebel movement a great boost and enabled Marxist rebels to dominate the leadership. With the help of Soviet, Chinese, Cuban and other Eastern bloc countries based in Aden, the capital of South Yemen, they intensified their efforts in the field while enjoying a safe haven in Aden.

Among the groups were the Dhufar Liberation Front (DLF) and the Popular Front for the Liberation of the Arabian Gulf (PFLOAG), which later became known as the Popular Front for the Liberation of Oman (PFLO). The first sought to detach Dhufar from Oman and establish a separate, Marxist state. The second had a grander design, which was to destabilize all Arab Gulf states and create radical and revolutionary regimes in those countries. Both groups operated training camps in South Yemen and were equipped and financed by communist countries and some Arab radical states.

By 1970, when the Sultan of Oman, Sa'id ibn Taymur, abdicated in favour of his son, the new Sultan Qabbus, both Saudi Arabia and Iran had become highly concerned over the success of the rebels and the threat they posed to Oman and to Gulf regional security. Saudi Arabia began providing financial aid to the Sultanate in mid-1971, and Iran soon followed suit by supplying military equipment. In 1973 the Shah became even more deeply involved by sending 30–35,000 fully equipped troops to Oman, accompanied by helicopters and artillery.[24] This move was widely seen at the time, particularly by the Gulf Arab states, as having more to do with Iran's intentions to be the predominant military power in the Gulf after the departure of the British than with helping against the rebels—another show of force such as his 1971 occupation of the three small islands belonging to the United Arab Emirates. Although the Iranian troops stayed in Oman for an extended period of time, they never militarily engaged the rebels.

Nevertheless, aided by the efforts of the Saudis and the Iranians (and the Jordanians who sent an engineer battalion), Oman was successful in defeating the radical forces in the region. Surprisingly, the Soviet Union was the first communist country to end its logistic and financial support of those radical movements. China and the other communist states followed suit in 1976 and 1977, respectively.[25]

Intelligence Co-operation
As already mentioned, prior to the overthrow of the Shah, Saudi Arabia and Iran shared a common fear of Soviet expansion in the region, either through direct military means or indirectly through proxies. Sharing a long border with the Soviet Union and having had Soviet troops on its soil, Iran under Shah Muhammad Riza was more conscious of the direct military threat. Saudi Arabia, on the other hand, was more concerned with the spread of atheistic communism, threatening the Islamic character of the region.

For the most part, the two countries' efforts against the Soviet communist threat were independent of each other. In one instance, however, they worked closely together. In 1974 Saudi Arabia and Iran joined with France, Egypt and Morocco in combating communism through multinational co-operation of the five countries' security services. The decision resulted in the creation of an anti-communist inter-security service group which aimed at tracking Soviet covert intelligence operations in the Gulf, the Third World and Europe. The group, which was given the code name the Safari Club, had no official headquarters, but its prime motivator was the French Intelligence Agency under Comte Alexandre De Marenches.[26]

Comte De Marenches was a staunch anti-communist who saw a worldwide communist threat and was determined to curb it through all available means. His approach was more political than military, i.e. based on enlightening the world community, particularly in Europe and the Third World, as to the dangers of communism. To do so, he needed the financial aid and logistical support that Saudi Arabia, Iran, Egypt and Morocco could provide. His arguments persuaded King Faisal to support him, which in turn enabled him to obtain the support of the other countries.[27] Despite its success, the Safari Club ceased its activities following the Iranian revolution of 1979 and the overthrow of the Shah. The new regime not only refused to co-operate in the common cause of fighting communism, but itself became one of the greatest threats to the political stability and internal security of the Gulf states.

Small or large, rich or poor, every modern nation-state needs its own intelligence service. The relationship between the intelligence services of Saudi Arabia and Iran was very limited since, in practical terms, there was no common ground for extensive co-operation. The goals, the tasks and even the tactics were very different. The revolutionary government of Iran chose its own version of security needs for the Gulf and chose to co-operate with some of the 'liberation movements' in the region. Post-1979 Iranian governments were also behind the creation of a number of terrorist organizations, both in the Middle East and in the Islamic world at large. Thus co-operation between the two countries on security matters came to an end, particularly after the outbreak of the Iran–Iraq war in September 1980.

In conclusion, despite some areas of co-operation, Saudi–Iranian military relations have always been sensitive and delicate. Historically, the two countries have pursued their own military needs with a minimum of co-ordination. Shah Muhammad Riza Pahlavi, and his father before him, were always keen to see Iran as the most powerful military power in the Gulf region. King Abd al-Aziz and his sons who succeeded him never intended to dominate the Gulf region militarily or build a modern offensive military force. Saudi military power has always been defensive and will continue to be so.

The era from the 1930s to the late 1970s witnessed numerous military understandings between Saudi Arabia and Iran, both productive and unproductive. Confrontational issues were inevitably resolved without a serious rupture in relations, and co-operation was encouraged wherever possible. Neither country was willing to see the expansion of communist influence into the Gulf, and there was a modest degree of co-operation to that end. And, despite their differences, neither country wanted hostilities. Nevertheless Iran undertook some provocative military actions in the Gulf during that period which could have had unpleasant military consequences. Military restraint on the part of Saudi Arabia, however, has always been an important factor in avoiding military conflicts in the region.

After the Iranian revolution, Saudi-Iranian relations have deteriorated considerably, and the Iran-Iraq war further strained military relations between the two countries. Saudi Arabia, however, was not a military participant in the war but had to take military precautions in order to defend itself against any potential military threat, particularly from Iran. As King Fahd, the Custodian of the Two Holy Mosques, reiterated many times, Saudi support for Iraq during its war with Iran was aimed at preventing Iran from defeating and invading Iraq and was not intended to defeat Iran. In the years following the war, Saudi-Iranian relations have stabilized. With mutual respect, they can continue to do so.

Appendix I. Friendship Treaty between the Kingdom of the Hijaz, Najd & its Dependencies and the Kingdom of Persia, 1929

Praise be to Allah alone and
Prayers and peace be upon the last of the Prophets;
We, Abd al-Aziz ibn Abd al-Rahman al-Faisal Al Saud King of the Hijaz, Najd & its Dependencies as we have concluded a 'Friendship Treaty' with His Majesty the Emperor of Iran with the view of establishing and strengthening the relations between our countries, which has been signed by two representatives on behalf of ourself and one representative on behalf of His Majesty the Emperor of Iran, the three who were equally entrusted with full authorization. The signing ceremony took place in the city of Tehran on:
18 Rabie al-Awwal 1348 (of Hijra)
2 Yur 1308 (Persian calendar)

Following is the operative text of the treaty:
Friendship Treaty
between
the Kingdom of the Hijaz, Najd & its Dependencies
and
the Kingdom of Persia
His Majesty the King of the Hijaz, Najd & its Dependencies
First Party; and
His Majesty the Emperor of Iran
Second Party

Upon mutual wish to establish and promote ties of friendship between the two countries; and

Believing that establishing these relations will serve the development of the two nations and help promote their welfare;

The two parties have decided to conclude a friendship treaty for this purpose:

His Majesty the King of the Hijaz, Najd & its Dependencies has appointed:
Sheikh Abdallah al-Fadhl
and Sheikh Muhammad Eid al-Rawwaf,
and His Majesty the Emperor of Iran has appointed:
His Excellency Haj Mahdy Qulli Khan Hedayat
the Prime Minister of Iran,

Appendices

as authorized representatives on behalf of them.

Upon examining their credentials, which proved to be identical to the original documents, the representatives agreed on the following articles:

Article I

Inviolable peace and sincere and durable friendship will reign between the Kingdom of the Hijaz, Najd & its Dependencies and the Empire of Iran, including the nationals of the two countries. The two contracting sides confirm their wish to exert all efforts to make such peace and friendship durable and to bolster the relations between them.

Article II

Whereas the two contracting parties rightfully wish to exchange Plenipotentiary Ministers and Consuls, they have agreed that the representatives of each party in the country of the other side will be accorded reciprocal treatment in accordance with the rules of international laws.

Article III

Both parties will extend to the nationals of the other party, while in their countries, all the rights and privileges extended to the nationals of the most preferred countries. The Government of the Kingdom of Hijaz, Najd & its Dependencies will also treat the Iranian pilgrims in all kinds of transactions on the same footing with other pilgrims. It will not put any obstacles in their way to observe their *hajj* rituals and religious obligations. It will, otherwise, facilitate for the pilgrims means of security, convenience and safety.

The two parties express their wish to add supplementary memorandums when the time is ripe for concluding agreements on political and economic matters.

Article IV

The original of this treaty has been signed in 4 copies in Arabic and Persian. The Arabic and Persian texts are to be regarded officially equally authentic.

Tehran: 18 Rabie al-Awwal 1348 (of Hijra)
2 Yur 1308 (Persian calendar)

(signed)   Abdallah al-Fadhl
(signed)   Muhammad Eid al-Rawwaf
(signed)   Mahdi Qulli

Appendices

Upon perusing and examining the foregoing treaty we have endorsed, accepted and authorized it as a whole and as articles and paragraphs. Therefore we endorse and conclude this treaty and give Royal Promise that we shall, God willing, execute and observe, quite honestly and sincerely, the items thereof. We shall, God willing, do our best to prevent any kind of violation of its rules.

Confirming the authenticity thereof we seal and sign this document before Allah, the best of all witnesses.

This treaty has been concluded at our palace on:
10 Jumada al-Thaniah 1348 (of Hijra)
AD 2 November 1929

Exchange of decrees of conclusion

The undersigned, fully authorized by their respective governments, met in the Foreign Affairs' Office in Jeddah for exchanging the decrees of conclusion of the friendship treaty between His Majesty the King of the Hijaz, Najd & its Dependencies and His Majesty the Shah-in-Shah of Iran which was signed in Tehran on:
18 Rabie al-Awwal 1348 (Hijra)
2 Yur 1308 (Persian calendar)
and concluded by the two governments in accordance with the ceremonies and procedures observed in the two countries.

Having verified the decrees of the concluded treaty which proved to be of one and the same content, the undersigned exchanged the decrees on this same day in accordance with the formal ceremonies observed.

In confirmation thereof the undersigned have put their signatures on this certification.

Written in Jeddah, this twelfth day of Muharram, one thousand three hundred and forty-nine.

(signed)　　Habibullah Hoveida
Representative of Iran in Jeddah

(signed)　　Fuad Hamsa
Undersecretary of Foreign Affairs

Appendix II. Text of Joint Communiqué at the Conclusion of the Visit of His Imperial Majesty the Shahinshah of Iran to Saudi Arabia, 1957

During the visit of His Majesty Muhammad Riza Shah Pahlavi, Shahinshah of Iran, to His Majesty King Saud of Saudi Arabia, 12–18 March, Their Majesties profited from the occasion to discuss various international issues in general and Middle Eastern problems in particular.

As a result of the exchange of views, agreement was reached on the following:

1. Their Majesties believe that the establishment of peace and security in the Middle East is directly dependent upon the establishment of peace and security in Palestine and that this cannot be achieved unless the legitimate rights of the Palestine Arabs are assured in accordance with the principles of justice and law in the framework of the United Nations.

2. All international disputes must be settled peacefully in accordance with the Charter of the United Nations and the use of force in any form and from any direction should be condemned.

3. The need for fostering and facilitating closer co-operation among Muslim states—whose best interest would be served, according to Islamic teachings and traditions, through united action to preserve the heritage of Islam and to defend moral principles against destructive ideologies and to continue such exchanges of views so that the mutual objectives can be achieved.

4. Their Majesties are very pleased to note that the efforts of the United Nations in the recent developments of the Middle East have been fruitful and believe that the more the foundations of this international organization are strengthened and its resolutions respected and complied with, the greater contribution will be made towards strengthening world peace and security; therefore they will never fail to support the United Nations.

5. Their Majesties believe that the awakening of the peoples spells the death of colonial policies and that to achieve genuine international relations based upon mutual respect for the freedom and independence of nations—which is the only basis for a true, lasting peace—the right of self-determination, which is one of the principles of the United Nations Charter, should be accepted and respected by all governments.

Riyadh, 18 March 1957

Appendix III. Commercial Agreement between the Kingdom of Saudi Arabia and the Kingdom of Iran, 1971

The Government of the Kingdom of Saudi Arabia and the Government of the Kingdom of Iran, desiring to develop, widen and strengthen the economic relations and in order to provide the necessary facilities for the commerce between their two countries on the basis of mutual benefits, agree on the following:

Article I

The two parties encourage the importation and exportation of goods and services between their countries, within the limits of the regulations and laws of both countries.

Article II

Desiring to encourage and to widen the scope of the commercial exchange between the two countries, each party authorizes the other to organize exhibitions in its country and will act to encourage such exhibitions, within the limits of the implemented regulations; both parties will also encourage the exchange of commercial delegations.

Article III

Payments related to the exportation and importation of goods between the two countries will be settled in US dollars, pounds sterling, or any other exchangeable currency agreed upon by the two parties.

Article IV

Both parties encourage, within the limits of the regulations and laws of their two countries, the private sector in both countries to implement joint ventures aiming at the development of industrial projects and projects of economic development, in order to provide for the needs of local and other markets.

Article V

The two parties agree on the constitution of a joint committee formed by representatives of the Kingdom of Saudi Arabia and the Kingdom of Iran, with the head of the representatives of both countries being on the level of Minister, with the following aims:

Appendices

1. Propose the means that will make possible the extension of the implementation of this Agreement.

2. Propose the necessary amendments to this Agreement.

3. Propose the ways and means of removing obstacles that could come in the way of the implementation of this Agreement.

The committee will meet alternately in Riyadh and Tehran, at least twice yearly.

Article VI

This Agreement will be implemented from the date of exchange of the ratified documents and will be effective for two years from that date; it will be renewed for a similar period upon the request of one of the parties and the written agreement of the other party.

The request for renewal will be presented at least three months before the end of this Agreement.
Made in Tehran on 18/2/1391 (Hijra)
25/1/1350 (Persian calendar)
In two original copies in Arabic and in Persian, both texts being of equal validity in interpreting their provisions.

On behalf of The Government of the Kingdom of Saudi Arabia	On behalf of The Government of the Kingdom of Iran

Notes

Chapter 1
1. See *The Kingdom of Saudi Arabia*, 6th ed. (Stacey International, London, 1983), pp. 81-2.
2. The movement is generally known in the West as Wahhabism after the founder, but his followers called themselves Muwahhidin or Unitarians. The word Imam has several meanings, all having religious connotations. Here it means leader of a nation of the faithful, known as the *ummah*.
3. For authoritative accounts of Saudi rule in the eighteenth, nineteenth and early twentieth centuries, see R. Bayley Winder, *Saudi Arabia in the Nineteenth Century* (St Martin's Press, New York, 1965) and Christine Moss Helms, *The Cohesion of Saudi Arabia* (Johns Hopkins University Press, Baltimore, Md., and London, 1981).
4. Abd al-Aziz initially kept the title of Sultanate of Najd since the aristocratic and deeply religious tribesmen of Najd took exception to the title of king, believing it demeaned the majesty and dominion of God.
5. Saeed M. Badeeb, *The Saudi-Egyptian Conflict over North Yemen, 1962-1970* (Westview Press/American-Arab Affairs Council, Boulder, Colo., and Washington, DC, 1986), p. 9.
6. Interview with Prof. R.K. Ramazani, Charlottesville, Va., Aug. 1988.
7. The same Shi'a clergy that opposed the destruction of the monarchy in the 1920s were behind the downfall of the Shah and the creation of an Islamic Republic in 1979.
8. Muhammad Hussein al-Aidarous, *Al-Alaqat al-Arabiah al-Iraniah, 1921-1971* (Arab-Iranian Relations, 1921-1971) (Dar al-Salasil Publications, Kuwait, 1985), p. 77.
9. Interview with Ramazani, Aug. 1988.
10. Badeeb, op. cit., p. 9.
11. Al-Aidarous, op. cit., p. 77.
12. Riza Shah (Khan) had conquered Tehran in a bloodless coup on 21 February 1921. He removed the previous government and appointed a new government headed by a well-known young journalist, Ziauddin Tabtabai, with himself as War Minister. Then, in October 1923, Riza Khan took over the premiership himself. See also al-Aidarous, op. cit., pp. 77-82.
13. It was located along the Shatt al-Arab and included most of Iran's oil industry.
14. Al-Aidarous, op. cit., p. 94.

Notes

15. Ibid., pp. 221-2.
16. The Iranian envoy to Cairo was also a non-resident envoy to the Saudi government before the 1929 Saudi-Iranian Friendship Treaty.
17. Al-Aidarous, op. cit., p. 223.
18. King Abd al-Aziz had to deal very sternly with his own fighters (the Ikhwan) when they tried to invade Iraq and Transjordan. In 1934, too, when his armies led by his sons were on the verge of conquering Yemen, he ordered them to withdraw.
19. Islamic law allows a man to have four wives concurrently. Divorce in order to acquire another wife was common in Abd al-Aziz's day and no stigma was attached to the former wife. On the contrary, it was an honour to be a former wife of the ruler.
20. Noel F. Bush, 'The King of Arabia', *Life* magazine, 31 May 1943, p. 71.
21. Ibid., p. 76.
22. Haleh Afshar, *Iran: A Revolution in Turmoil* (State University of New York Press, New York, 1985), pp. 81-2.
23. Ibid.
24. Ibid.
25. David E. Long, 'Iran', in David E. Long and Bernard Reich (eds), *The Government and Politics of the Middle East and North Africa* (Westview Press, Boulder, Colo., 1980), p. 74.
26. Ibid.
27. Afshar, op. cit., pp. 82-3.
28. Abdel Aati Mohamed Ahmed, *The Saudi Diplomacy in the Gulf and the Arabian Peninsula* (Cairo, Center for Political and Strategic Studies, El-Ahram, 1979), p. 73.
29. For more details, see Mohammed Mohsen Ali Asaad, 'Saudi Arabia's National Security: A Perspective Derived from Political, Economic, and Defense Policies' (unpublished PhD dissertation, Faculty of Claremont Graduate School, 1981).
30. Ibid., p. 241.
31. Ibid., p. 252.
32. Ibid., p. 256.
33. Badeeb, op. cit., p. 9.
34. Asaad, op. cit., p. 261. See also R.K. Ramazani, *Revolutionary Iran: Challenge and Response in the Middle East* (Johns Hopkins University Press, Baltimore, Md., and London, 1987), p. 4.
35. Asaad, op. cit., p. 262.
36. For more details and later treaties and agreements between Iraq and Iran concerning the Shatt al-Arab, refer to ibid., pp. 262-4. See also Majid Khadduri's book on territorial disputes.
37. Assad, op. cit., pp. 264-5.

Notes

38. Salim Wakim, *Iran, The Arabs, and the West* (Vantage Press, New York, Atlanta, Los Angeles, Chicago, 1987), p. 137.

39. Stephen C. Pelletiere, *The Kurds: An Unstable Element in the Gulf* (Westview Press, Boulder, Colo., and London, 1984), p. 15.

40. George Lenczowski, *Soviet Advances In the Middle East* (American Enterprise Institute for Public Policy Research, Washington, DC, 1971), p. 23. In 1941 a Soviet–British agreement was reached allowing the two countries to occupy Iran to assure war supplies from the West to Russia.

41. Ibid.

42. Ibid., p. 24.

43. Miron Rezum, *The Soviet Union and Iran* (Westview Press, Boulder, Colo. and London, 1988), p. 139.

44. Ibid., pp. 139-40. Many Iranians today consider that Herat belongs to Iran and was given by the British to Afghanistan (interview with Ambassador Ja'far Raed [last Iranian ambassador to Saudi Arabia during the reign of Mohammed Riza Shah], London, March 1988).

45. Rezum, op. cit., p. 139.

46. Al-Aidarous, op. cit., pp. 221-2.

47. Ibid., pp. 260-70.

48. Sir Gilbert Clayton, ed. by Robert O. Collins, *An Arabian Diary* (University of California Press, Berkeley and Los Angeles, 1969), p. 111.

49. Badeeb, op. cit., p. 9.

50. Clayton, op. cit., p. 42.

51. Ibid., p. 111; al-Aidarous, op. cit., p. 77.

52. Clayton, op. cit., p. 42.

53. Ibid.

54. Ibid.

55. Ibid., p. 120.

56. Ibid.

57. Ibid., pp. 122-3.

58. Iran also has a significant minority of Sunni Muslims, found mostly among the Kurds, Baluchis and Arabs living along the southern coasts, and also among the Turkoman tribes in northern Khorassan. See *Iran Almanac*, 7th ed. (1968), p. 329.

59. *Encyclopedia of Islam*, Vol. I, p. 155.

60. David E. Long, *The Hajj Today: A Survey of the Contemporary Makkah Pilgrimage* (State University of New York Press, Albany, 1979, in co-operation with the Middle East Institute), pp. 130-1.

61. After the fall of Makkah to Ibn Saud, King Hussein of the Hijaz abdicated the throne and went into exile at Aqaba. His son Ali was named King and remained in Jeddah, which was under siege by Saudi forces. See also *Encyclopedia of Islam*, Vol. I, pp. 153-4.

Notes

62. Habibollah Khan Hoveida was the father of Amir Abbas Hoveida who served as Prime Minister of Iran for 13 years during the reign of Mohammed Riza Shah Pahlavi.

63. See text of declassified confidential telegram No. E 5059/3704/91, dated 4 Oct. 1929, from the British representative in Tehran to the Foreign Office in London (Public Record Office, London).

64. See confidential report No. E 4426/104/34, dated 3 Sept. 1929, from Sir R. Clive, the British representative in Persia, to Mr A. Henderson, the Principal Secretary of State for Foreign Affairs (Public Record Office, London).

65. See text of declassified confidential report No. E 4426/104/34, dated 24 Aug. 1929, from the British representative in Tehran to the Secretary of State for Foreign Affairs. The report was based on Intelligence Summary No. 17 compiled by the British military attaché in Tehran (Public Record Office, London).

66. Interview with Ambassador Raed, March 1988.

Chapter 2

1. Only King Fouad of Egypt did not recognize King Abd al-Aziz in 1932. He even severed diplomatic relations with the Kingdom of Saudi Arabia. King Fouad's action was attributed to his ambitions to establish Cairo as the capital of the Islamic Caliphate with Makkah and Madinah (the two holy cities in Islam) as subordinate to Egypt.

2. With the introduction of women's education in the 1960s, women have participated more in various social activities. Women now work in education as teachers and are administrators of girls' schools; and in the health field they work as doctors and nurses.

3. Fouad al-Farsy, *Saudi Arabia: A Case Study in Development*, 2nd ed. (Stacey International, London, 1980), pp. 63-7, 89-96.

4. David E. Long, 'Iran' in David E. Long and Bernard Reich (eds), *The Government and Politics of the Middle East and North Africa* (Westview Press, Boulder, Colo., 1980), p. 77.

5. John W. Limbert, *Iran: At War With History* (Westview Press, Boulder, Colo., 1987), Table 2.1, p. 21.

6. Miron Rezum, *The Soviet Union and Iran* (Westview Press, Boulder, Colo., & London, 1988), p. 79.

7. Ibid., p. 81.

8. Ibid., p. 79.

9. Ibid., p. 171.

10. Under Islamic law and according to Arab traditions and customs, the public acceptance of and allegiance to a leader through general consensus is called *bay'ah* or *mubay'ah*.

11. Lenczowski, op. cit., p. 171.

Notes

12. Al-Farsy, op. cit., p. 93.
13. Ibid., p. 32.
14. Khayr al-Din al-Zarkali, *Shibh al-Jazirah al-Arabiah fi Ahd al-Malik Abd al-Aziz* (The Arabian Peninsula during the Time of King Abd al-Aziz), 2nd ed. (Dar al-Ilm lil-Malayeen, Beirut, 1982), Vol. I, p. 571.
15. Ibid.
16. Ibid., p. 419.
17. Ibid., p. 443.
18. Lenczowski, op. cit., p. 419.
19. Long, op. cit., p. 74.
20. Rezum, op. cit., pp. 260-1.
21. Majid Khadduri, *Arab Contemporaries: The Role of Personalities in Politics* (Johns Hopkins University Press, Baltimore, Md., and London, 1973), p. 88.

Chapter 3

1. Even before the creation of the Kingdom, Abd al-Aziz and Riza Shah had signed a Friendship Treaty and established diplomatic relations in 1929.
2. Jacob Goldberg, *The Foreign Policy of Saudi Arabia: The Formative Years, 1902–1918* (Harvard University Press, Cambridge, Mass., and London, 1986), p. 174.
3. The first Saudi dynasty was from 1744 to 1818. The second Saudi dynasty was from 1824 to 1865.
4. Khayr al-Din al-Zarkali, *Shibh al-Jazirah al-Arabiah fi Ahd al-Malik Abd al-Aziz* (The Arabian Peninsula during the Time of King Abd al-Aziz), 2nd ed. (Dar al-Ilm lil-Malayeen, Beirut, 1982), Vol. I, pp. 540-56.
5. Interview with Prof. R.K. Ramazani, University of Virginia, Aug. 1988.
6. See text of treaty in Appendix I of the present book.
7. See Telegram No. E 6322/3704/91, dated 10 Nov. 1929, from Mr Bond to Mr Butler (Public Record Office, London).
8. Interview with Ambassador Ja'far Raed, London, March 1988.
9. Although many Iranians made the pilgrimage to Makkah and Madinah, Riza Shah never did during his lifetime. Ironically, his remains did visit the two holy shrines when they were conveyed from Cairo to Tehran through Saudi Arabia. Riza Shah abdicated the throne in 1941 following the Allies' occupation of Iran. He died in exile in South Africa in 1944. His body was first buried in Cairo and then moved in 1949 to Tehran. See also Ja'far Raed, 'Highlights on the Saudi–Iranian Relationship', unpublished paper (in Arabic), London, 1988.
10. Riza Shah's personal admiration of Hitler's autocracy and ultra-nationalism may have contributed to suspicions that his neutrality would not extend deeply. See Dilip Hiro, *Iran Under the Ayatollahs* (Routledge, London and New York, 1987), p. 29.

11. *Um Ul-Qora* (newspaper), no. 990, 20 Dhu al-Hija 1362 AH (= 17 Dec. 1943) (Official Notice, No. 82).

12. Ch. 4, which deals with Saudi–Iranian religious relations, explores the details of this incident.

13. No. 77 H/162.

14. Translated text of the Saudi Foreign Ministry's letter No. 20/1/4, dated 29 Dec. 1943.

15. Translated text of letter No. 77 H/186, dated 2 Feb. 1944, from the Iranian Embassy in Saudi Arabia to the Saudi Foreign Ministry.

16. A declassified ciphered telegram No. 592, dated 7 Oct. 1944, from the British Embassy in Jeddah to the British Foreign Office in London (Public Record Office, London).

17. King Abd al-Aziz's letter to Shah Mohammed Riza Pahlavi was carried by Adel Bek Ossayran, a well-known Lebanese politician.

18. Saudi Arabia appointed Hamja Ghoth as its first ambassador to Iran, and Tehran appointed Abd al-Hassein Sadig Isfandiari as its minister to Saudi Arabia (interview with Ambassador Raed, March 1988).

19. Mozaffar Alam was a high-ranking Iranian dignitary who served as acting Foreign Minister during the reign of Riza Pahlavi. See Ja'far Raed, 'History of Iran–Saudi Relations', *Rouzegare-Now* (London), summer 1988.

20. Chapter 5, which deals with economic relations, contains a full discussion of the oil issue.

21. The Egyptian monarchy was overthrown in 1952 when the Free Officers succeeded in their bloodless coup. As one of the Free Officers, Nasser became Egypt's absolute ruler and began his Nasserist movement, aimed at destroying all monarchies in the Middle East and establishing an all-Arab unity, i.e. pan-Arabism, under his leadership.

22. Saudi Arabia was among the founding member states who signed the San Francisco agreement announcing the birth of the United Nations in 1945. Iran was not a founding member but joined the UN on 24 October 1945.

23. The Baghdad Pact was signed in 1955 by Iraq, Pakistan, Turkey, Iran and Britain, with the United States as an observer.

24. See declassified confidential telegram No. EP 10325/1, dated 3 May 1956, from Tehran to London (Public Record Office, London).

25. See declassified cipher telegram No. 406, dated 25 April 1956, from the British Embassy in Tehran to the Foreign Office in London (Public Record Office, London).

26. See declassified confidential telegram No. 1062/1/56, dated 19 Jan. 1956, from the British Residency in Bahrain to the Foreign Office in London (Public Record Office, London).

27. Interview on 17 Aug. 1989 with Harry Kern, foreign editor of *Newsweek* in the 1950s and director of Private Advisory Inc., based in Washington, DC (see

Notes

note 38 to the present chapter). Kern reported that the Shah's attitude apparently changed as his career progressed. He notes one occasion on which about 100 peasants assembled outside the Marble Palace in Tehran to receive deeds to land. Each peasant, as he received the deed, bent down and kissed the Shah's feet.

28. The Buraimi oasis issue was finally resolved in 1974, when King Faisal and Sheik Zayd of the UAE signed an agreement in Jeddah under which the two countries agreed to share oil revenues from the oasis. See also David Holden and Richard Johns, *The House of Saud* (Holt, Rinehart & Winston, New York, 1981), p. 145.

29. See declassified confidential telegram No. 1622/4/56, dated 22 Feb. 1956, from the British Embassy in Tehran to the Foreign Office in London (Public Record Office, London).

30. Princess Fawziah was the first wife of Shah Mohammed Riza Pahlavi and their marriage was political (interview with Kern, Aug. 1989).

31. Saudi Arabia severed its diplomatic relations with Britain and France as a result of the tripartite invasion of Egypt in 1956. The first Arab oil embargo was also imposed on Britain and France by Saudi Arabia. Iran continued its oil shipments.

32. See declassified cipher No. 406, dated 25 April 1956, from the British Embassy in Tehran to the Foreign Office in London (Public Record Office, London).

33. See declassified confidential report No. 36 dated 23 March 1957, from the British Embassy in Tehran to the Foreign Office in London (Public Record Office, London).

34. Ibid.

35. Britain viewed the Shah's idea of a Saudi–Iranian defence pact as a threat to the British-protected sheikhdoms in the Gulf. Therefore, the British favoured a Saudi–Iranian–Iraqi defence pact against communism, since they knew that Saudi Arabia would not join the Baghdad Pact. See declassified secret report No. 37, dated 28 March 1957, from the British Embassy in Tehran to the Foreign Office in London (Public Record Office, London).

36. Ibid., p. 2. Saudi–British diplomatic relations were resumed in 1963 after Nasser's invasion of North Yemen in September 1962.

37. See full text of the communiqué in Appendix II of the present book.

38. See *Foreign Reports Bulletin* (henceforth *FRB*), 18 May 1959. *Foreign Reports Bulletin* is a publication of Private Advisory Inc., based in Washington, DC, and run by Harry Kern and his son Nathaniel Kern. It is a highly respected and recognized bulletin in US government circles and in many Middle Eastern as well as Asian countries such as Japan.

39. Iraq under the republican regime decided to withdraw from the Baghdad Pact in 1959, a move which meant the death of the pact.

40. The question concerning Iran's recognition of Israel was asked by the editor and editorial writer of *Kayhan* newspaper, one of the two most important papers in Tehran. See *FRB*, 22 Aug. 1960.
41. The United Press correspondent in Tehran was an Iranian Jew who was suspected of working with the Israelis. See ibid.
42. Ibid., 28 July 1960.
43. Egypt was in a union with Syria at the time. Known as the United Arab Republic (UAR), it was promulgated in 1958, but ceased to exist in 1961 when Syria withdrew.
44. *FRB*, 25 Aug. 1960.
45. Ibid., 5 Aug. 1960.
46. Throughout the years of Saudi–Iranian diplomatic relations (1929–79), Saudi Arabia appointed only 3 ambassadors to Iran. Iran, on the other hand, appointed 13 ambassadors to Saudi Arabia between 1930 and 1979. See article by Ambassador Ja'far Raed in *Al-Sharq al-Awsat* newspaper, 28 April 1988, p. 5.
47. Interview by *FRB*'s chief editor with Iran's Prime Minister Ali Amini on 11 April 1962 (*FRB*, 17 April 1962).
48. A detailed account of the two countries' military assistance to the ex-Imam of Yemen and his royalist followers is given in Ch. 6 of the present book, which analyses military relations. The North Yemen problem lasted for eight years (1962–70). For a full account of this conflict, see Saeed M. Badeeb, *The Saudi–Egyptian Conflict over North Yemen, 1962–1970* (Westview Press/American–Arab Affairs Council, Boulder, Colo., 1986).
49. *FRB*, 28 Nov. 1962.
50. Ibid., 6 July 1964.
51. Interview with Prof. R.K. Ramazani, Charlottesville, Va., Aug. 1988.
52. *FRB*, 9 Feb. 1964.
53. The assassination attempt against the Shah was carried out by a soldier named Riza Shamsabadi who was stationed in the rear of the Marble Palace as part of the detachment of the Imperial Guard assigned to duty inside the palace compound. As the Shah entered his ground floor office, the assassin came around the corner of the palace firing his sub-machine-gun, burst through the palace door and fired on two plain clothes guards. They returned fire as the assassin sprayed the hallway with bullets. One bullet passed through the door of the Shah's office and fell near his desk. Both guards and the assassin were killed in the exchange of fire. It was later discovered that the assassination attempt was a Chinese communist plot. For more details, see ibid., 14, 29, 30 April 1965.
54. Ibid., 6 Feb. 1965.
55. The Iranian Parliament was holding two vacant seats for representatives of Bahrain, which it considered as an Iranian lost province. The Bahraini issue, however, was resolved in 1971 as a result of an agreement reached by King Faisal and the Shah of Iran.

Notes

56. *Iran Almanac*, 4th ed. (1964–65), p. 236.
57. Ibid., 6th ed. (1967), p. 219. A final pact on the Continental Shelf was signed between the two countries on 24 Oct. 1968, in Tehran.
58. Ibid., p. 253.
59. Ibid.
60. Interview with Shah Mohammed Riza Pahlavi, 30 March 1966 (*FRB*, 6 April 1966).
61. The Jewish governor of New York was supposed to host a dinner for King Faisal during his June 1966 visit to the United States. However, the governor cancelled the dinner party after the King's public attack on zionism and communism during a Washington press meeting.
62. *Iran Almanac*, 6th ed. (1967), p. 253.
63. *FRB*, 12 Jan. 1966.
64. Only recently, under the Khomeini regime, has Iran applied for membership of the non-aligned movement. Shah Mohammed Riza Pahlavi was always proud of Iran's pro-Western stand. The non-aligned movement was the brainchild of India's first post-independence Prime Minister, Jawaharlal Nehru, who proposed it in 1956 but substituted it with the idea of anti-colonialism in 1961. However, the idea of non-alignment re-emerged in 1963 when Nehru, Josep Tito of Yugoslavia and President Nasser of Egypt convened and officially formed the movement.
65. *FRB*, 9 Dec. 1966.
66. *Iran Almanac*, 7th ed. (1968), p. 236.
67. Ibid.
68. A Saudi official who prefers to remain anonymous.
69. More details of this issue are included in the discussion of Saudi–Iranian military relations in Ch. 6.
70. *Iran Almanac*, 7th ed. (1968), p. 236.
71. Ibid.
72. For the historical record, when Shah Mohammed Riza Pahlavi was forced to leave Iran in 1979, it was the Arabs, the people he always mistrusted, who welcomed him in Egypt where he eventually died and is buried. His European and American friends, whom he trusted, refused to guarantee him a residence visa.
73. Nazir Fansa, *Teheran: The Fate of The West* (Jacques Arakel Publications, Paris, 1988), p. 79. Also a personal interview with Nazir Fansa by the author, Paris, April 1988.
74. Interview with Fansa, April 1988.
75. *Iran Almanac*, 8th ed. (1969), p. 216.
76. Interview with Fansa, April 1988. He also mentioned this historical event in his book, *Teheran: The Fate of the West*, op. cit., p. 80. The phrase 'Amir

al-Muminin', or 'Prince of Believers', is a highly respected title which was given to the early Caliphs and successors of the Prophet Muhammad.

77. *Iran Almanac*, 8th ed. (1969), p. 215.
78. Interview with Ambassador Raed, April 1988.
79. *FRB*, 6 March 1970.
80. Ibid., 5 Nov. 1979.
81. Ibid., 15 April 1968, p. 2.
82. In March and July 1971, the Shah gave interviews to correspondents of Associated Press and the Indian magazine *Blitz*, where he renewed his threats of occupying the islands of Abu Musa, and the Greater and Lesser Tunbs. Consequently, those statements overshadowed developments in the Gulf.
83. *FRB*, 9 Nov. 1971, p. 4, and 2 Dec. 1971.
84. Details of the invasion are discussed in Ch. 6.
85. Muhammad Hussein al-Aidarous, *Al-Alaqat al-Arabiah al-Iraniah, 1921–1971* (Arab–Iranian Relations, 1921–1971) (Dar al-Salasil Publications, Kuwait, 1985), pp. 392-408.
86. Ibid., pp. 427-8.
87. See text of agreement in ibid., p. 428.
88. Bahrouz Souresrafil, *Khomeini and Israel*, 2nd ed. (C.C. Press, UK, 1989), p. 26.
89. *Iran Almanac*, 4th ed. (1975), p. 164.
90. A Saudi diplomat who prefers to remain anonymous.
91. David E. Long, 'Saudi Arabia and the Horn of Africa', unpublished paper (Feb. 1990), p. 1.
92. A Saudi intelligence officer who prefers to remain anonymous.
93. *Arab News*, 30 April 1975. This Saudi–English newspaper published a special issue on 25 April 1975, analysing the forthcoming visit of the Shah to the Kingdom.
94. *Golden Register for Magnificents* (Dar al-Ray al-Am, Vol. 1, Cairo, 1978), pp. 193-4.
95. Until the overthrow of the Shah, Iran was an active member of the Qods, i.e. Jerusalem Islamic Committee. The Committee was formed by the heads of Islamic nations during the first Islamic Conference in Rabat in 1969. It is responsible for keeping track of the situation in Jerusalem under Israeli occupation and is currently headed by King Hassan II of Morocco.
96. *FRB*, 18 Nov. 1977.
97. Court Minister Assadollah Alam had served as Iran's Prime Minister in 1963. He was the son of a tough tribal chief from eastern Iran and had been a close friend of the Shah since boyhood. When in 1963 Iran faced similar riots to those of 1978, Alam ordered the army to fire into the mobs who had begun raging throughout central Tehran. Many people were killed but order was

Notes

immediately restored. Alam died of leukaemia in April 1978 in New York. See also *FRB*, 10 Aug. 1977 and 12 May 1978.

Chapter 4

1. M.H. Qureshi, *Islamic Jurisprudence* (Nafis Publications, Karachi, 1970), pp. 22-9.
2. Ibid., p. 21.
3. Dr Ahmad Muhammad Ahmad Jili, *A Study on the Sects in the History of the Muslims* (in Arabic), 2nd ed. (King Faisal Centre for Research and Islamic Studies, 1988), pp. 151-3.
4. Ibid., pp. 179-81.
5. This claim was reiterated by Ayatollah Khomeini, the leader of the 1979 revolution in Iran, before his death.
6. Nikki R. Keddie, 'The Roots of the Ulama's Power in Modern Iran', in Nikki R. Keddie (ed.), *Scholars, Saints and Sufis* (University of California Press, Berkeley, Los Angeles, and London, 1978), pp. 222-4. The current Iranian regime follows the Usulis school. In his book *Vilayat al-Faqih* (The Rule of the Learned), Ayatollah Khomeini wrote that it is the learned person (the *faqih*) who must be the Imam of the people until the hidden Twelfth Imam reappears.
7. *Muslim Journal, An International Magazine*, L-No. 8254 (Sept. 1989), p. 29.
8. Ibid., pp. 21-2.
9. *The Kingdom of Saudi Arabia*, 7th ed. (Stacey International, London and New Jersey, 1986), p. 77.
10. Ibid.
11. The Roman Empire was the second superpower of the time.
12. The second Muslim Caliph, Omar Ibn al-Khattab, is hated by the Iranians, even today, because of his conquest of Persia. Nowadays one cannot find any Iranian with the name of Omar.
13. Muhammad Husayn Haykal, *The Life of Muhammad*, transl. from the 8th edn by Isma'il Ragi A. al-Faruqi (Cairo, 1979), pp. 365-6.
14. Nadir Shah of the Qajars was an anti-mullah ruler who deprived them of one of their sources of income, namely, the *waqf* (endowment). His unrealized aim was to curb the mullahs' power and influence. See Keddie, op. cit., pp. 225-6.
15. Dilip Hiro, *Iran Under the Ayatollahs* (Routledge, London and New York, 1987), pp. 22-4.
16. Ibid., p. 25.
17. The SAVAK was established in 1955. In Farsi, it is called Sazman-e Amniyat Va Ittilaat-e Keshvar, i.e. Organization of National Security and Intelligence. In fact, it was a police intelligence organization.

Notes

18. From the mid-eighteenth century, the Saudi royal family, in co-operation with the religious Islamic revival movement of Sheikh Muhammad ibn Abd al-Wahhab, has had control over the two holy cities of Makkah and Madinah.

19. Before King Abd al-Aziz's capture of the Hijaz Kingdom, including the two holy cities of Makkah and Madinah, it was impossible for travellers and pilgrims to reach the holy shrines without being robbed, looted or even killed.

20. Sir Gilbert Clayton, ed. by Robert O. Collins, *An Arabian Diary* (University of California, Berkeley and Los Angeles, 1969), pp. 112-20.

21. When Muslims all over the world perform their prayer five times a day, they face the Ka'bah, which is located inside the Great Mosque in Makkah. The Ka'bah was built by Abraham, the father of Prophets, and his son Isma'il. It is a cube-shaped structure measuring 13m x 11m x 16m. In the north-east corner of the Ka'bah is the black stone which is said to be one of the stones of heaven. Not far from the Ka'bah lies the stand of Abraham where his footprints can be seen.

22. Interview with Dr Salim Wakim, a Lebanese historian and former journalist who now lives in Geneva, 29 Oct. 1990.

23. *Encyclopedia of Islam*, Vol. I, p. 154. The same evening, the people of Hijaz expressed their favourable feelings to the statement of the King by saying, 'We acknowledge you, Sultan Abd al-Aziz, as King of the Hijaz in accordance with the Holy Book and the *Sunna* of the Prophet...Makkah will be the capital and we shall be under your protection.'

24. *Encyclopedia of Islam*, Vol. I, p. 155. Iran sent 3,403 pilgrims (*hajjis*) that year. See also David E. Long, *The Hajj Today: A Survey of the Contemporary Makkah Pilgrimage* (State University of New York Press, Albany, 1979, in co-operation with the Middle East Institute), pp. 130-1.

25. Long, op. cit., p. 1. All *hajj* services are now carried out by very sophisticated intergovernmental agencies. The Saudi Ministry of Hajj and Endowment, in co-operation with those agencies, is totally responsible for the *hajj* affairs. Other Saudi ministries such as the Ministry of Health, the Ministry of PTT and the Ministry of Interior, also render their services during the *hajj* season.

26. Interview with Ambassador Ja'far Raed, London, March 1988.

27. These figures have been acquired on a personal basis by the author from the Assistant Deputy Minister for Pilgrimage Affairs, Makkah, 1989.

28. In 1988 the Foreign Ministers of the Islamic world decided during their summit meeting in Amman, sponsored by the Organization of the Islamic Conference (OIC), that only 10 per cent of the total population of each Muslim country is allowed to make the annual pilgrimage to Makkah. Since the total population of Iran is approximately 45 million, therefore, and according to the OIC decision, only 45,000 Iranian pilgrims are allowed to make the annual

pilgrimage. Iran, which did not participate in the summit, refuses to accept and adhere to that decision.

29. Interview with a retired Saudi Security General who witnessed those incidents, but wishes to remain anonymous, Riyadh, Feb. 1990.

30. Ibid.

31. Ibid.

32. When Ayatollah Khomeini came to power in Iran in 1979, he issued a *fatwa* permitting Iranian pilgrims and other Shi'as to follow the Sunni Imams of the two holy mosques during prayer time. He also ordered Iranians to perform the *salat* of Jum'ah (Friday) in all the mosques of Iran. These may be two positive actions taken by Khomeini during his lifetime towards uniting the Muslim *ummah*.

33. Interview with a leading Iranian Sunni living in exile in Paris and who wishes to remain anonymous, Paris, 20 March 1988.

34. *Al-Manhal* (Saudi monthly magazine) (Jeddah), Vol. 27, Dec. 1965, p. 671.

35. Anthony Parsons, *The Pride and the Fall, Iran 1974–1979* (Jonathan Cape, London, 1984), p. 25.

36. The Pakistani Islamic Brotherhood Association was created in Karachi in 1948, one year after the creation of the Islamic Republic of Pakistan.

37. The Organization of the Congress of the Islamic World still exists, with its headquarters in the city of Karachi. It is one of the three major Islamic organizations operating in the Islamic world today.

Chapter 5

1. For a discussion of *hajj* receipts during this period, see David E. Long, *The Hajj Today: A Survey of the Contemporary Makkah Pilgrimage* (State University of New York Press, Albany, 1979).

2. A British government monthly payment to King Abd al-Aziz was in the range of £5–10,000. At the end of March 1924, the British ceased to subsidize the King. See declassified British document on Arabia 1918–1928, Ch. 9, p. 33.

3. *The Kingdom of Saudi Arabia* (Ministry of Information, 1987) (in English, French and German), p. 26. The settlements programme was further expanded during the reign of King Faisal (1964–75).

4. On Saudi television, King Fahd recently recounted a story, told to him by his father, King Abd al-Aziz, many years ago. King Abd al-Aziz used to visit an old woman in the community, and as he prepared to leave, the old woman would raise her hand and pray that Allah would open up for him 'the treasures of the earth'. The King could never imagine what treasures the old woman was talking about until oil was discovered. Then he recalled her prayers.

5. David E. Long, *The United States and Saudi Arabia: Ambivalent Allies* (Westview Press, Boulder, Colo., 1985), pp. 12-16.

Notes

6. Petromin and Samarec are the two other oil companies in the Kingdom of Saudi Arabia.

7. Saudi Arabia, Royal Decree No. 30/4/1/1047 of 25 Rajab 1371 AH (20 April 1952). See also Arthur N. Young, *Saudi Arabia: The Making of a Financial Giant* (New York University Press, New York, 1983).

8. See confidential telegram No. 42, dated 12 March 1952, from the British Embassy in Jeddah to the Foreign Office in London (Public Record Office, London).

9. Arthur N. Young, 'Economic Review: Saudi Arabian Currency and Finance', pt. 2, *Middle East Journal* 7, no. 4 (1953), p. 547.

10. *The First Development Plan* (Ministry of Planning, Riyadh, 1970), p. 10.

11. John W. Limbert, *Iran: At War With History* (Westview Press, Boulder, Colo., 1987), p. 11. The name was ultimately changed to British Petroleum after Iran nationalized its oil resources in 1951.

12. Fred Halliday, *Iran: Dictatorship and Development* (Penguin Books, New York, 1979), pp. 140-1.

13. Ibid., p. 143.

14. 'Economy of Iran in the Past Ten Years', unpublished economic report prepared by the Iranian Embassy in Bonn, Jan. 1991, p. 5.

15. Ibid., p. 9.

16. Ja'far Raed, 'The Iranian Economy Two and One Half Years After the War', *Al-Mujaz*, edition no. 11, 2nd year (London), March 1991, pp. 15-20.

17. See minutes of the Fifth Meeting of the British Sub-committee on the Persian Gulf, 24 Oct. 1928 (a declassified secret document at the Public Record Office, London).

18. Ibid.

19. See Great Britain, India Office, *Slavery in the Persian Gulf*, revised, Sept. 1928 (BRO), pp. 135-40. The Iranians included a specific minor reservation, or *ad referendum* to the League convention. This means that they wanted the League to set a time for their full control over their territorial waters.

20. Ibid., p. 136.

21. Ibid., p. 138.

22. In 1962 a Saudi Royal Decree was issued banning the trade of slavery and awarding freedom to all slaves living in the Kingdom. Similar measures were taken by other Gulf states.

23. The treaty was signed in Tehran in 1929. For the text, see Appendix No. 1, Saudi Arabian Ministry of Foreign Affairs, *Collection of Treaties, 1922-1951*, 5th ed., Makkah (al-Banawi Enterprises, Jeddah), pp. 44-6.

24. *Iran Almanac* (1973), p. 158.

25. Among the most famous families who acted as agents and representatives for Iranian merchants in the Kingdom are the Alireza, Zeinal and Asfahani families. In addition to their commercial role, these families acted as hosts and

organizers for the Iranian pilgrims during the *hajj* season and for visits to the holy shrines in Makkah and Madinah during the rest of the year.

26. Trevor Mostyn, *Major Events in Iran, Iraq and the Arabian Peninsula (1945-1990)* (Facts on File, New York/Oxford, 1991), p. 1.

27. Lee E. Preston and Karim A. Nashashibi, *Trade Patterns in the Middle East* (American Enterprise Institute [AEI], Washington, DC, Oct. 1970), pp. 50-1.

28. Ibid., p. 51.

29. Ibid., p. 17. Saudi Arabia is a country that respects and adheres to any bilateral or multilateral agreements that it signs. History has proved that the Kingdom has never violated its agreements with other parties and in many cases has insisted on implementing those agreements in full.

30. Ibid., p. 19.

31. See cable No. 36, confidential, from Sir Roger Stevens in Tehran to Mr Selwyn Lloyd at the Foreign Office, London, 23 March 1957, concerning the Shah of Iran's visit to Saudi Arabia; and the full text of the joint communiqué that was issued after the visit, p. 3. See also App. II of the present book.

32. *Iran Almanac*, 7th ed. (1968), p. 391.

33. This was a major Saudi concession. Saudi policy stipulates that the Saudi airline splits the charter *hajj* air traffic with carriers from the country of origin. If that country does not wish to carry its half, Saudia will do so and pay the country a royalty on its share. Conversely, Saudia should receive a royalty for its share carried by the other carriers. Iran had long insisted it carry all its *hajjis* without making any payments to Saudia.

34. *Iran Almanac*, 10th ed. (1971), pp. 224-5.

35. Ibid., p. 225.

36. Ibid., 11th ed. (1972), p. 244.

37. *FRB*, 11 May 1971, p. 1.

38. Ibid.

39. Richard Chadbourn Weisberg, *The Politics of Crude Oil Pricing in the Middle East, 1970-1975: A Study in International Bargaining*, Research Service No. 31 (Institute of International Studies, University of California, Berkeley, Calif., 1977), p. 78.

40. HIM Mohammed Riza Pahlavi Aryamehr Shahanshah of Iran, *The White Revolution*, 2nd ed. (The Imperial Pahlavi Library, Kayhan Press, Tehran, Aug. 1967), p. 24.

41. *FRB*, July 1969, p. 2.

42. Interview with an Iranian diplomat who chose to stay in the United States after the 1979 Iranian revolution, Washington, DC, 31 August 1988.

43. *FRB*, 18 Oct. 1974, p. 2. It was reported at the time that the Saudi Oil Minister was not able to play any role in this new approach to Iran due to the intense hostility shown towards him by the Iranians from the Shah down.

44. *Iran: Foreign Policy Series*, No. 2 (1974), p. 32. See also *Iran Almanac*, 12th ed. (1973), p. 158.
45. *Iran Almanac*, 14th ed. (1975), p. 156.
46. From the author's private papers.

Chapter 6
1. *The Arab Bulletin of the Arab Bureau in Cairo, 1916-1919*, Vol. IV, 1919 (Archive Ed., London, 1986), pp. 86-7.
2. In his article, 'The Empire Shrinks Back' (*Times Literary Supplement*, 16 Aug. 1991, p. 8), W.M. Roger Louis writes, 'Over a period of 150 years the sheikhs had surrendered to the British the conduct of external affairs in return for protection against aggression. The British in internal matters gave only advice, sometimes heeded by the sheikhs, but often not.'
3. Muhammad Hussein al-Aidarous, *Al-Alaqat al-Arabiah al-Iraniah, 1921-1971* (Arab-Iranian Relations, 1921-1971) (Dar al-Salasil Publications, Kuwait, 1985), pp. 224-6.
4. Ibid. See also details of this issue in Ch. 1 of the present book.
5. Al-Aidarous, op. cit., p. 222.
6. See details of this visit in Ch. 3 of the present book.
7. Declassified report No. 406, dated 23 March 1957, from the British Embassy in Tehran to the Foreign Office in London (Public Record Office, London).
8. Before leaving the Gulf in 1971, the British had wanted all the lower Gulf sheikhdoms, Bahrain, Qatar and the former Trucial States—Abu Dhabi, Dubai, Sharjah, Ras al-Khaymah, Fujayrah, Ajman, and Umm al-Quwayn—to unite in a single country, which they thought would be a more viable state. Bahrain and Qatar decided not to join, but the Trucial States became the United Arab Emirates. Shah Mohammed Riza Pahlavi opposed the federation but, faced with reality, he had to recognize it.
9. In 1881 and again in 1904, Persia had tried to occupy these islands, but was rebuffed by the British.
10. *FRB*, 27 July 1991.
11. Interview with Harry Kern, editor of *FRB*, 23 Sept. 1991.
12. Anthony Cordesman, *The Gulf and the Search for Strategic Stability* (Westview Press, Boulder, Colo., and Mansell, London), pp. 164-5.
13. Ibid.
14. Letter to the author from Harry Kern, dated 4 Jan. 1988.
15. Ibid.
16. In essence, the Baghdad Pact was the brainchild of Nuri al-Sa'id, Iraq's Prime Minister at the time. Accused by the new revolutionary regime of Iraq of being a stooge of the British government and an Arab traitor, he was brutally killed during the revolution, being dragged through the streets of Baghdad while

Notes

tied to a moving car. Members of the Hashimite royal family were also brutally massacred, including women and infants.

17. *Majalat al-Tadamun al-Islami* (Islamic Solidarity Magazine), published by the Saudi Arabian Ministry of Hajj and Awqaf, special edn, Sept. 1991, pp. 6-21.

18. For more details on Saudi–American relations, see David E. Long, *The United States and Saudi Arabia: Ambivalent Allies* (Westview Press, Boulder, Colo., 1985), pp. 33-69.

19. Cordesman, op. cit., pp. 725-8.

20. See declassified document No. EP 10325/3, dated 2 April 1957, from R.B. Stevens, the British representative in Tehran, to the British Foreign Office.

21. Ibid.

22. Ibid.

23. Ibid.

24. Cordesman, op. cit., pp. 431-7.

25. Ibid., pp. 432-9.

26. From the author's private papers.

27. Comte Alexandre De Marenches, who headed the French Intelligence Organization (DGSE) from 1970 to 1981, was called 'The Prince of Secrets' by the European media. In 1986 he broke his silence about his role in the Safari Club, agreeing to interviews in three major European magazines in which he spoke of his experiences in combating communism and working with other countries. See *Le Point*, no. 728 (Sept. 1986), *L'Express* (5 Sept. 1986) and *Der Spiegel*, no. 37, Vol. 8 (Sept. 1986).

Index of Names

Abadan 28
Abd al-Aziz ibn Abd al-Rahman Al Saud (Ibn Saud), King of Saudi Arabia 13, 17, 19–52 *passim*, 75–6, 79–82, 85, 94–6, 102, 103, 115–19, 127, 128, 131
Abd al-Rahman Al Saud, Amir 19
Abdallah ibn Abd al-Aziz Al Saud, Crown Prince of Saudi Arabia 117
Abdallah ibn Jilawi Al Saud, Amir 44
Abu Bakr 77, 85
Abu Dhabi 26–7, 53
Abu Hanifa No'man ibn Sabit, Imam 71
Abu Musa 30, 62, 63, 120–1
Abu Saafa 26
Aden 59, 123, 129
Afghanistan, Afghans 29–30, 94
Africa 65, 67, 70, 108
Agha Khan, Prince 73
Akhbaris 73
Alam, Assadollah 67, 120–1
Alam, Mozaffar 51
Algiers Agreement 28
Ali, King of the Hijaz 35
Ali ibn Abi Talib 72–3, 85
Amanullah Khan, King of Afghanistan 29–30
America *see* US
American University of Beirut 109
Amini, Ali 56
Amouzegar, Jamshid 64, 67
Anglo-Persian (later Anglo-Iranian) Oil Company 98
Angola 65
al-Aqsa mosque 89
Arab–Israeli war [1967] 60, 66, 83, 107, 111
Arab–Israeli war [1973] 64
Arab League 55, 56, 105
Arabi [island] 122
Arabia, South 59
Arabian American Oil Company *see* ARAMCO
Arabian Sea 126
Arabistan 21–2, 117, 118; *see also* Khuzistan
Arafat, Mount 85
Aram, Abbas 58
neo-Aramaeans 39
ARAMCO (Arabian American Oil Company) 96, 104, 109
Armenians 39
Aryans 39
Asir 20, 21, 27, 94, 116
Assyrians 39
Ataturk (Mustafa Kemal) 20, 21, 98
Azerbaijan, Azerbaijanis 39, 41, 123
Azeris 39

al-Badr, Muhammad, Imam of Yemen 56, 59, 129
Baghdad 25, 35, 51, 55, 102, 123
Baghdad Pact 52–3, 54, 55, 123–4
Bahrain 22, 26, 30, 48, 53, 58, 60, 61, 62–3, 102, 118–21

157

Index

Baku 45
Baluchistan, Baluchis 39, 103
Bandar Abbas 110
Bank Melli Iran 104
Baqi' graveyard [Madinah] 86
Ba'thism 69
Beirut 55, 109
Britain (United Kingdom), British *passim*
Buhman, Mirza Ali Akbar Khan 33
al-Buraimi 26-7, 53, 54

Cairo 22, 31, 53, 118
California Arabian Standard Oil Company *see* CASOC
Carter, President Jimmy 67, 112
CASOC (California Arabian Standard Oil Company) 96
Caspian Sea 29
CENTO (Central Treaty Organization) 58, 124
Central Treaty Organization *see* CENTO
Cham'oun, Camille, President of Lebanon 54
China, Chinese 65, 108, 129, 130
Chosroes, Emperor of Persia 76
Christianity 69-70
Clayton, Sir Gilbert 33-4
Communist Party of Iran (Hezb-e Komonist-e Iran) 45; *see also* Tudeh Party
Cox, Sir Percy 25
Cuba, Cubans 65, 129
Cyrus, Emperor of Persia 76

Damascus 33, 73, 77, 80, 105
Dammam No. 1 oilwell 96
Dammam No. 7 oilwell 95, 96
D'Arcy, William Knox 98
al-Dar'iyah 75

al-Dawasir tribe 116
al-Dawish, Faisal 26, 116
Dhahran 53
Dhufar 129-30
Dhufar Liberation Front *see* DLF
DLF (Dhufar Liberation Front) 130
Dubai 102
Dutch East Indies 97

Eastern Province [Saudi Arabia] 38, 44, 94, 102, 104, 116
Egypt, Egyptians 31, 33, 34, 51-6 *passim*, 59, 62, 65, 66, 68, 75, 77, 79, 80, 82, 123, 128, 129, 130-1
Erzurum Treaty 28
Esso (EXXON) 96
Ethiopia 61
Euphrates 28
Europe, Europeans 48, 49, 65, 70, 96, 108, 110, 123, 131
Eve, tomb of 34

al-Fadl, Abdallah 35
Fahd ibn Abd al-Aziz Al Saud, Crown Prince (later King) of Saudi Arabia 66, 112, 126, 132
Faisal ibn Abd al-Aziz Al Saud, Crown Prince (later King) of Saudi Arabia 22, 39, 44, 46, 47, 49, 57-66, 87-9, 97, 107, 110-12, 116, 119-20, 129, 131
Farouq, King of Egypt 53
Farsi [island] 122
Fatima 72
Fawziah, Princess 53
Fedaiyan-e Islam 78
Fertile Crescent 52
Foreign Reports Bulletin 56, 120

Index

Fouad, King of Egypt 31, 34, 79
France, French 20, 44, 65, 97, 112, 123, 130-1

GCC (Gulf Co-operation Council) 124
Geneva 62
Germany, Germans 20, 22, 24, 49, 123
Gilan 29, 123; Gilanis 39
Goldberg, Jacob 47
Gulf, the Arabian *passim*
Gulf Co-operation Council *see* GCC

Ha'il 19, 44
Hamadan 102
Hanafi school 71
Hanbali school 34, 38, 41, 72, 75, 81, 95
Harb tribe 116
al-Hasa 38, 94, 101, 102
Hashimite dynasty 33, 80, 124
Hassan [son of Ali] 73
Herat province 30
Hezb-e Komonist-e Iran (Communist Party of Iran) 45
Hijaz 19-21, 23-4, 31, 33-4, 39, 42-3, 44, 75-6, 80-3, 94, 96, 101-2, 104; *see also* Hijaz, Najd and its Dependencies, Kingdom of the
Hijaz, Najd and its Dependencies, Kingdom of the 16, 20-1, 35, 103
Hinjam 30
Holmes, Major Frank 96
Hormuz, Strait of 30, 120
Hoveida, Amir Abbas 58, 67
Hoveida, Habibollah Khan 33, 35
Hussein [son of Ali] 72-3
Hussein, King of Jordan 55

Hussein, Sherif of Mecca and King of the Hijaz 31, 35, 116

ibn Hanbal, Imam Abu Abdallah Ahmad 72
ibn Mahfuz, Salim 97
Ibn Saud *see* Abd al-Aziz ibn Abd al-Rahman Al Saud
Ibn Taymiyya, Sheikh 75
al-Idrisi 21
Igbal, Dr Manuchehr 61
Ikhwan (Muwahideen) 23, 24, 25, 26, 31, 75, 116
Imam Muhammad ibn Saud University [Riyadh] 126
Imperial Airways 102
India 58, 103, 108, 123
Indian Ocean 121
Indo-Europeans 39
Indonesia 70, 97
Iran (Persia), Iranians (Persians) *passim*
Iran Air 85, 107
Iran Almanac 93
Iran-Arab Friendship Association 58
Iran-Iraq war [1980-88] 18, 28, 90, 100-1, 113, 118, 125-6, 131, 132
Iraq, Iraqis 15, 25-6, 27-8, 29, 51, 54, 55, 59, 62, 66, 86, 102, 123-4, 127; Iraq-Iran war *see* Iran-Iraq war
Islam *passim*; *see particularly* Ch. 4
Islamic Common Market 90, 107
Isma'ilis 73
Israel 53, 55-6, 57, 60, 64, 65, 66, 67, 89, 105-7, 111, 122, 123; *see also* Arab-Israeli wars
Israeli Military Industries 122

Index

Issa, Hamad ibn 119
Issa, Muhammad ibn 119

Ja'farrya (Twelver) sect 44
Japan, Japanese 57, 70, 108
al-Jazirah Bank 104
Jeddah 22, 30, 33–5, 49, 54, 61, 80, 89, 97, 104, 116, 118
Jerusalem 66, 67, 69, 77, 89
Jews 39, 48, 105
Jizan 21, 27
Jordan 58, 60, 66, 129, 130
Jubail 98
Judaism 69

Ka'bah 31, 50, 80, 85
al-Ka'ki 97
Karachi 88, 102
Karbala 86
Kashani, Ayatollah 85
Kashmir 58
Kern, Harry 120–1
Khalid ibn Abd al-Aziz Al Saud, King of Saudi Arabia 47, 65–6, 112
Khawr al-Udayd 27
Khaz'al, Sheikh 21, 118
Khomeini, Ayatollah Ruhollah 47, 67, 68, 79, 91, 113
Khorramshahr *see* Muhammara
Khorrasan 41
Khrushchev, Nikita 125
Khuzistan 21, 28, 39; *see also* Arabistan
Kuchek Khan 29
Kurdistan 41
Kurds 28–9, 39, 123
Kuwait 15, 16, 22, 25, 26, 30, 59, 60, 66, 118

League of the Islamic World 89
League of Nations 22, 28, 30, 103, 118
Lebanon, Lebanese 51, 54, 56, 92, 105
Lebinah, Greater 26
Lebinah, Lesser 26
Lend-Lease aid 96, 104, 127
Libya 77
Long, Dr David E. 83
Lurs 39

Madinah 19, 31, 33–5, 49, 54, 58, 69, 73–6, 79-83, 85, 86, 91, 97, 116
Mahabad 123
Makkah 19, 20, 23, 31, 33–5, 49, 50, 54, 58, 69, 74–6, 79–86, 89, 91, 97
Malik ibn Anas al-Arabi, Imam 72
Maliki school 71–2
Mansur ibn Abd al-Aziz Al Saud, Prince 116
Marenches, Comte Alexandre De 131
Marxism 129, 130
Mauritania 70
Mazandaranis 39
Mediterranean 65, 105
Mo'awiyah ibn Abi Sufyan 73
Mobil 96
Moguls 70
Mojahedin-e Islam 78
Morocco 61, 65, 66, 129, 130–1
Mossadeq, Muhammad 65, 78, 99, 105, 127
Muhammad Ali Pasha 75, 79
Muhammad ibn Abd al-Aziz Al Saud, Prince 116
Muhammad ibn Abdallah, the Prophet 31, 38, 69–76 *passim*, 80, 81, 85, 86, 116
Muhammad ibn Saud, Amir of al-Dar'iyah 75

Index

Muhammad Riza Shah Pahlavi 16, 20, 22, 45, 47–68 *passim*, 78–9, 86–90 *passim*, 99–101, 104, 107–13 *passim*, 119–21, 122, 124, 126–31 *passim*
Muhammara (Khorramshahr) 28; Treaty of 25
Mujtahids *see* Usulis
al-Muntazar, Muhammad 73
Muslim World League 89
Mutayr tribe 116
Mu'tazilites 73
Muwahideen *see* Ikhwan

Nadir (Nasser al-Din) Shah 77
Naif ibn Abd al-Aziz Al Saud, Prince 66
Najd (Central Arabia); Sultanate of Najd and its Dependencies 19–21, 25, 26, 31, 37, 39, 43, 75, 84, 94, 101, 116; *see also* Hijaz, Najd and its Dependencies, Kingdom of the
Najran 21, 27
Nasser, President Gamal Abd-al 52, 54–8 *passim*, 60, 66, 129
National Guard [Saudi Arabia] 117
National Iranian Oil Company *see* NIOC
National Liberation Movement [Iran] 45
Navai, Afrassial 56
Nazi Germany 20, 22, 24, 48
Netherlands Trading Society 97
New York 59
New Zealand 96
Nice 65
NIOC (National Iranian Oil Company) 61, 99, 107, 108, 109
Nixon Doctrine 61, 124
Noah 69

OIC (Organization of the Islamic Conference) 62, 89, 90
Oman 22, 26–7, 30, 53, 102, 103, 118, 121, 123, 129–30
Omar ibn al-Khattab 77, 85, 118
Omayyad dynasty 73
OPEC (Organization of Petroleum Exporting Countries) 57, 64, 66, 67, 107–13
Organization of the Congress of the Islamic World 88
Organization of the Islamic Conference *see* OIC
Organization of Petroleum Exporting Countries *see* OPEC
Ottoman Empire 20, 28, 75; *see also* Turkey
Oyaynah 75

Pahlavi dynasty 16, 21, 92; *see also* Muhammad Riza Shah Pahlavi; Riza Shah Pahlavi
Pakistan, Pakistanis 39, 58, 73, 94, 123
Pakistani Islamic Brotherhood Association 88
Palestine, Palestinians 33, 48, 54, 59, 61, 66, 67, 80, 105
Paris 21, 79, 122
Persia (Iran), Persians (Iranians) *passim*
PFLO (Popular Front for the Liberation of Oman) 130
PFLOAG (Popular Front for the Liberation of the Arabian Gulf) 130
Popular Front for the Liberation of the Arabian Gulf *see* PFLOAG
Popular Front for the Liberation of Oman *see* PFLO
Pushtuns 29

161

Index

Qabbus, Sultan of Oman 130
Qajar dynasty 20, 21, 42, 77, 78, 98, 117; *see also* Nadir (Nasser al-Din) Shah
Qashqa'is 39
Qasimi islands 120
Qatar 22, 30, 109, 118, 121
al-Qatif 38, 94
Qawasim tribe 120

Rabat 61, 65, 89
Rafsanjani, Hashemi 101
Ras al-Khaymah 120
Al Rashid dynasty 19, 44, 116
Rastakhiz (Resurgence) Party [Iran] 45
Red Army 29
Red Sea 16, 19, 50, 94, 98
Riyadh 15, 54, 57, 58, 75, 116, 126, 128
Riza Khan *see* Riza Shah Pahlavi
Riza Shah Pahlavi (Riza Khan) 13, 16, 17, 20–49 *passim*, 77–83 *passim*, 98–9, 102–5 *passim*, 115–19 *passim*, 123, 127, 128, 131
Roman Empire 77
Russia, Russians 16, 28, 29, 30, 45, 50, 77, 123, 125; *see also* USSR

Sa'ad al-Faisal Al Saud, Prince 107
Saddam Hussein 15, 69
Safari Club 131
Safavid Empire 77
al-Saggaf, Sayyed Omar 59, 64
Sa'id ibn Taymur, Sultan of Oman 130
SAMA (Saudi Arabian Monetary Agency) 97
Al Saud dynasty 19, 26, 31, 35, 43, 44, 75; *see also* individual members
Saud al-Faisal Al Saud, Prince 64, 67, 112
Saud ibn Abd al-Aziz Al Saud, King of Saudi Arabia 52–5, 87, 116, 119, 124
Saudi Arabia *passim*; *see also* Hijaz, Najd and its Dependencies, Kingdom of the
Saudi Arabian Airlines 85, 107
Saudi Arabian Bank 97
Saudi Arabian Monetary Agency *see* SAMA
SAVAK 59, 78
Sevener Shi'ism 73
al-Shafa'i, Muhammad ibn Idris 72
Shafa'i school 72
Shah Bahar base 126
Shari'a 20, 42, 50, 70, 72, 73, 75, 76, 85
Sharjah 63, 120
Shatt al-Arab 28, 29
Al al-Sheikh family 43, 44
Shi'a 17, 20, 22, 34, 38, 41, 44, 70–3, 79, 84–8, 90, 92, 99, 100, 119, 125; *see also* Twelver Shi'ism
Sibilla, Battle of 24, 26
Sidon 105
Socal (Standard Oil of California) 96
Somalia 65
South Africa 108
Soviet Union, Soviets *see* USSR
Standard Oil of California *see* Socal
Stevens, R.B. 128
Stockholm 112
Subai' tribe 116
Sudan 58

Index

Suez crisis 53, 54
Sultan ibn Abd al-Aziz Al Saud, Prince 66, 117, 121
Sunna 38, 71, 75
Sunnis 17, 34, 37, 39, 42, 70-3, 77, 84, 86-7, 99
Switzerland 54
Syria 29, 54, 128

Taif 65; Treaty of 27
TAPLINE (Trans-Arabian pipeline) 104-5
Tehran 21, 35, 39, 49, 51, 53, 55, 57, 58, 59, 61, 64, 65, 78, 79, 102, 108, 112, 113, 117, 119, 122, 126, 128
Texaco 96
Tigris 28
Trans-Arabian pipeline *see* TAPLINE
Transjordan 25
Trucial Coast 103
Trucial States 27, 30, 48, 120; *see also* UAE
Tudeh Party [Iran] 29, 65
Tunbs, Greater and Lesser 30, 62, 63, 120-1
Turkey 20, 21, 28, 29, 30, 52, 98, 110, 123; *see also* Ottoman Empire
Turkistan 41
Turkomans 39
Turks 70
Tusan 75
Twelver Shi'ism 41, 44, 73, 77; Twelvers 41, 73
Twin Pillar Policy 124, 127

UAE (United Arab Emirates) 27, 30, 53, 109, 120, 130
UAR (United Arab Republic) 55-6
UN (United Nations) 22, 26, 52, 53, 63, 119-20, 136
Union of Soviet Socialist Republics *see* USSR
United Arab Emirates *see* UAE
United Arab Republic *see* UAR
United Kingdom *see* Britain
United Nations *see* UN
United Press 55
United States *see* US
Uqayr 25
US (United States) 13, 14, 29, 48, 49, 51, 59, 60, 61, 63, 64, 65, 67, 69, 70, 78, 96, 97, 108, 111, 112, 122-4, 127, 128
USSR (Union of Soviet Socialist Republics) 16, 29, 41, 49, 54, 58, 60, 65, 69, 105, 123-31 *passim*; *see also* Russia, Russians
Usulis (Mujtahids) 73
Utaybah tribe 116

Venezuela 108

Wadi Sirhan 25
al-Wahhab, Sheikh Muhammad ibn Abd 19, 31, 34, 43, 75, 81
Wahhabi movement 23, 26, 38, 41, 43, 75, 76, 81, 116
Washington 15, 16, 120
West, the; Westerners 13, 14, 16, 18, 19, 29, 41, 44, 48, 51, 52, 54, 58, 60, 63-4, 67, 70, 72, 78, 88, 91, 97, 99, 102, 123-5, 127
Western Province [Saudi Arabia] 97
White Revolution [Iran] 99-100, 110

Yahya, Imam of Yemen 27
Yamani, Sheikh Ahmad Zaki 63,

64, 109
Yanbu' 98
al-Yazdi, Hajji Abu Talib 85
Yemen 27, 59, 76, 116; North Yemen 56, 58, 59, 73, 129; South Yemen 27, 59, 123, 125, 129–30

Zahedi, Ardashir 62, 120, 122
Zayd, Imam 73
Zaydis 73
Zoroastrianism 77